Shaped by the Word

258 N. Merton
Memphis, TN 38112

THE MEMPHIS SCHOOL
OF SERVANT LEADERSHIP

Shaped by the Word

THE POWER OF SCRIPTURE
IN SPIRITUAL FORMATION

M. Robert Mulholland, Jr.

THE UPPER ROOM
Nashville, Tennessee

Cover design: Harriette Bateman
Book design: Roy Wallace
Eighth printing: 2000

Library of Congress Catalog Card Number: 85-51241
ISBN: 0-8358-0519-0

Printed in the United States of America on acid-free paper

Lovingly dedicated to

Lynn, Jeremy, and Tareena,
Viola and Richard,
the Lord's gracious community
for my spiritual formation

Contents

Foreword by Rueben P. Job *11*

Preface *13*

I. Introduction
1. Getting Oriented *17*
2. How to "Read" without "Reading" *21*
3. The Nature of Spiritual Formation *27*

II. Focal Perceptual Shifts
4. Various Words of God *33*
5. Information Versus Formation *47*
6. The Iconographic Nature of Scripture *61*
7. Kairotic Existence *69*

III. Focal Experiential Shifts
8. Functional-Relational Dynamics *83*
9. Being and Doing *95*

IV. **The Power of Scripture in Spiritual Formation**
10.   Breaking the Crust   *109*
11.   Wesley's Guidelines for Reading Scripture   *119*
12.   Obstacles to Spiritual Reading   *129*
13.   The Practice of Spiritual Reading   *139*

Appendix A   Spiritual Formation and Psychology   *159*

Appendix B   Excerpt from the Preface to Wesley's
Notes on the Old Testament   *165*

Notes   *167*

Shaped
by the
Word

Foreword

THE transforming power of God is available to every Christian. But the transformed life does not come by accident or by chance. To be formed in Christ and to have Christ formed within us is clearly a gift of God. And yet, there are requirements made of us if we are to receive the gift of transformation.

Many fail to receive this gift because they have not been carefully taught. We have done little to teach persons how to receive the transforming power of God into their lives or how to live their lives within the transforming presence of God. Many of us begin our spiritual pilgrimage without much awareness of the resource that is available to us in the Bible.

Clearly, one of the most important resources for spiritual formation is the Bible. But our approach to the Bible will in large measure determine its transforming effect upon our lives. Dr. Mulholland's clear distinction between information and formation is a very helpful concept for the person serious about spiritual formation. He points out the poverty of any informational approach to spirituality. Often our desire to know is simply another expression of our consumptive culture, of our acquisitive nature, of our desire to have more and more and more. The approach to the scriptures suggested by Dr. Mulholland is radically different from an informational approach.

The enormous interest in spiritual formation today is a symptom of humankind's deep hunger for God. This yearning for God holds great promise and potential for another great awakening and for a world more loving and just. This time also holds great risk. The temptation to offer cheap grace, an easy way, a sure answer, a success oriented program is always with us. Bob Mulholland offers the kind of direction that can save us from turning our hunger for God into another fad. Here is a resource that can keep us moving toward the One who continually urges us onward in our pilgrimage toward wholeness, maturity, perfection, spiritual formation, God.

One of the great strengths of this volume is that it grows out of the spiritual pilgrimage of a capable and committed biblical scholar. The academic homework has been done, and the serious student will not be disappointed. It was my privilege to hear these lectures when they were presented to the Academy for Spiritual Formation. They became for those who heard them a window to God. May this volume be as much for you, the reader.

RUEBEN P. JOB
Bishop, Iowa Area
United Methodist Church

Preface

THIS book emerged from a week of lectures delivered to the initial gathering of The Academy for Spiritual Formation, launched by The Upper Room in May, 1983. Following the lectures, Bishop Rueben P. Job, then World Editor of The Upper Room, requested that the lectures be prepared for publication as quickly as possible.

A heavy load of administrative as well as teaching responsibilities made it impossible for me to give attention to the project at that time. In order to facilitate the process, Ms. Janice T. Grana, the present World Editor of The Upper Room, offered to have the tapes of the lectures transcribed. For this invaluable assistance, I am indebted to Ms. Grana and the unknown people who undertook the tedious task of transcribing many hours of lectures.

I am also indebted to Ms. Grana and Ms. Marie L. Roy, who took Ms. Grana's place as editor for this project when Ms. Grana was elected World Editor. Their support, encouragement, and advice has been most helpful, to say nothing of their understanding when it became impossible to meet the first deadline that had been agreed upon.

Finally, this book would have been delayed even longer had it not been for the many, many hours my family sacrificially released for me to work upon this project. Most of all, I must acknowledge the painstaking work of proofreading and correcting undertaken by my wife Lynn and her mother, Viola Scholl.

I.

INTRODUCTION

Getting Oriented

*A*S I listen to people across the country wrestle with the dynamics of spiritual formation, I repeatedly hear the following terms: adventure, search, hunger, journey, quest, pilgrimage. There is an awakening in the church to the need for spiritual formation as an essential part of growth into Christian wholeness. Increasingly, more and more programs of spiritual formation are appearing, more and more books on the spiritual journey are being written. Many of these are profound and rich; others, unfortunately, superficial and simplistic.

I do not claim to be an expert in the experience of spiritual formation. In fact, there probably aren't any "experts" in this field. We are all fellow pilgrims on the way toward the wholeness God has for us in Christ. We build one another up as we share with each other what we have encountered, what we have experienced, what we have learned in our pilgrimage.

It is my prayer that this book might be whatever God wants it to be in your life. I don't know what God purposes to do in your life through this book; probably you don't know either. I doubt if we ever really know completely and fully, in any sort of comprehensive way, exactly what God wants to do in our life at any given point. But God *does* have purposes. Ultimately, you are not reading this book simply because you want to read it for some personal reason, although you certainly have a personal reason. Far deeper than whatever motivation led you to open this book are the purposes God wants to fulfill in your life, and this book may very well be part of those purposes. I pray that together we will let the Lord fulfill those purposes.

As we begin, I would ask you to covenant with me in prayer: first, pray for me, that what I write will be released to God for you; second, pray that you will be released to God as you read so that God can speak to you through me; third, pray that you will be yielded to whatever it is God wants to do in your life through this book. Take a couple of moments, right now, to center down. I don't know what you have been doing for the past few hours. Perhaps you have been abiding in God's presence. More likely, you have been fragmented and disturbed by the various pressures of your life. Take a few moments to center down in silence. In whatever way you release yourself to God, take time to release yourself and to give God permission to do whatever he wants to do with you in your reading of this chapter. You may want to join me in this prayer:

> *Lord, we thank you for your divine providence in our lives that has so ordered the course of our living that you have brought us to be intertwined together in this book. We pray that by your grace, by the deep working of your Spirit in our lives, you would help us to be so released to you in what we do together that you may be able to fulfill in us and through us the good and perfect will for our wholeness for which you have brought us together in this book. In the name of Jesus we pray. Amen.*

One of the difficulties in preparing a book like this is not knowing where you, the reader, are in your experience and practice of Christian spirituality. This means that some of what I have to say may be familiar to you. In this case, perhaps God's reason for your reading this book is to give you a spiritual discipline of patient endurance; although, as one of our New Testament fathers in the faith has said, it doesn't hurt to hear again some of the basics (Phil. 3:1). If you find I am going over things that seem to be at the beginning level of spirituality, I hope you will see it as an opportunity for offering to God a spiritual discipline of patient endurance.

There may be other things I feel led to share with you which may be disturbing, upsetting, or troubling to you. Let me say at the outset this is not my intended purpose or goal. But if you do find this happening, I would suggest that perhaps those are the points where God is seeking entrance into your life at a deeper level. That disturbance, that upsetting element, that troubling idea may be God's knock upon one of the closed doors of your life. I have discovered in my own spiritual life, as I hope you have, that most often when I run into something which is destructive to my inner peace, very frequently it is the beginning of God's knock upon some area of my life where I have closed God out and imprisoned myself within.

We usually think of Revelation 3:20, where Jesus speaks of knocking, as God's knock upon the unrepentant sinner's heart. We must remember that this letter was addressed to *Christians*. True, they were lukewarm, worldly, acculturated Christians. They were Christians who had accommodated themselves to the values, perspectives, and dynamics of the surrounding culture (Rev. 3:15–17). They were Christians who were shutting God out of their lives in the world. However, God was standing at those closed doors in their lives and knocking. God says to them, "Those whom I love, I reprove and nurture" (Rev. 3:19).[1]

When God puts a "finger" on those things in our lives which are inconsistent with God's will for our wholeness, it is not simply to point them out. It is not just to say that they must go or must be changed. That finger has a hand attached that offers us the nurture into wholeness which we need at that point. This is the essential nature of God's knocking upon the closed doors of our lives. God knocks at those points where he is shut out of our lives and we are imprisoned within, imprisoned by some bondage which does not allow us to be free in God's love and in God's will

19

for our wholeness in our life with others. Precisely at these points in my life is where I regularly encounter something that disturbs me, upsets me, troubles me, throws me off balance in either my perceptions or my feelings. With consistent regularity, these experiences become God's knock upon the closed doors of my life. These are the points where God chooses to begin a new work of wholeness in my being.

I suggest to you that if you become disturbed with what I share with you in this book, perhaps, instead of tuning me out or turning me off or giving up the book, your first reaction should be to consider the possibility that God may be knocking upon some door in your life.

Finally, it may initially appear that the direction in which I am approaching the topic is rather circuitous. You may be expecting me simply to give you information or techniques or methodologies or models on *how* to use the scripture in spiritual formation; and I will discuss all these in the latter chapters of the book. But perhaps the "how" is more radical than you realize. Perhaps the "how" is not so much a body of information, a technique, a method, or a model as it is a *mode of being* that we bring to the use of the scripture in spiritual formation. Perhaps any technique or method or model, in and of itself, becomes unfruitful and can even become damaging if we do not approach the scripture in that mode of being which will allow us to be formed spiritually by it. Thus, before we can consider the techniques, the methods, the models for the use of scripture in spiritual formation, we must first examine that mode of being which enables us effectively to employ them as means of God's transforming power in our daily lives.

2.

How to "Read" without "Reading"

T HE moment you opened this book to read, a powerful set of preconditioned dynamics of perception
went into operation. You are the "victim" of a lifelong, educationally enhanced learning mode that establishes *you* as the controlling power (reader) who seeks to
master a body of information (text) that can be used by you
(technique, method, model) to advance your own purposes (in this case, spiritual formation).

We have a deeply ingrained way of reading in which *we*
are the masters of the material we read. We come to a text
with our own agenda firmly in place, perhaps not always
consciously but usually subconsciously. If what we start to
read does not fairly quickly begin to adapt itself to our
agenda, we usually lay it aside and look for something that
does. When what we are reading does adapt itself to our
agenda, we then exercise control over it by grasping it with
our mind. The rational, cognitive, intellectual dynamics of
our being go into full operation to analyze, critique, dis-
sect, reorganize, synthesize, and digest the material we
find appropriate to our agenda. Thus our general mode of
reading is to perceive the text as an object "out there" over
which we have control. *We* control *our* approach to the text;

21

we control *our* interaction with the text; *we* control the impact of the text upon *our* lives.

This mode of reading is detrimental to the role of scripture in spiritual formation.[1] In fact, it is but one facet of a whole mode of being that militates against all genuine spiritual formation. This is why the "how" of spiritual formation is perhaps more radical than you realize. This is why the "how" of the use of scripture in spiritual formation is not so much a body of information, a technique, a method, a model, as it is a mode of being that we bring to the scripture.

In the light of this situation, I would like to suggest to you an alternate mode of learning, specifically an alternate mode of approach to reading.

First, I suggest that your top priority be to listen for God. Seek to allow your attention and focus to be on listening for what God is saying to you as you read this book. Listen for God to speak to you in and through, around and within, over and behind and out front of everything that you read. Keep asking yourself, "What is God seeking to say to me in all of this?" By adopting this posture toward the text you will begin the process of reversing the learning mode that establishes *you* as the controlling power who seeks to master a body of information. Instead, you will begin to allow the text to become an instrument of God's control in your life. You will begin to open yourself to the possibility of God's setting the agenda for your life through the text. Not only will this exercise begin to transform your approach to reading (and prepare you for the use of scripture in spiritual formation), it will also begin to transform your whole mode of being in a way that will enhance all genuine spiritual formation.

Second, I suggest that you respond to what you read in this book with your heart and spirit rather than with your rational, cognitive, intellectual dynamics. Now, in saying this, I am sure that you are in no danger of neglecting those cognitive, rational, analytical dynamics of your being. They are so hyper-developed in our culture and in our normal modes of learning that we are not going to have to worry about getting them out of balance. The problem is that we are over-balanced in that direction, and we tend to think that this is proper—the sharper you are intellectually, the smarter you are, the more brilliant you are, the more quickly you can grasp concepts and integrate and synthesize them, the more balanced you are.

I am not sure this is the case, not when we are talking about wholeness of being. Yes, we must love God with all of our mind. We must seek to utilize our cognitive, intellectual, rational dynamics to the best of our ability. We cannot shirk this at all. However, we must remember that the injunction to love God with all of our mind comes a little bit farther down the road in Jesus' list; loving God with all of our heart and all of our soul precedes loving God with all of our mind. Our predominant mode, however, *is* the rational, the cognitive, the intellectual. We filter, we sift everything through the cognitive processes of our mind.

I am not saying that there is anything wrong with this mode of operation; but there is an imbalance in the role of the rational, cognitive dynamics in our lives. The problem with such an imbalance is that it enables us to stand back from whatever we encounter, to stand independent of it, to evaluate it in the light of our own best judgment, and then make some kind of decision on how we are going to deal with it. Can you see the problem that arises here? What if it is God who is meeting us in whatever we encounter? What if we stand back in our purely cognitive, rational, intellectual mode of operation; evaluate the encounter in the light of our own best interest as we see it (even enlightened Christian best interest); and determine that what we are encountering is not for us? If we do this, and it is a predominant tendency in our lives, we are insulating that "door" of our being against the "knock" of God. Why? We are not really opening our being at deeper levels to the possibility of God's being in that encounter.

Adopting an alternate mode of approach to your reading is going to be difficult. You will find yourself struggling against this imbalance in your life. You are going to find yourself constantly leaning toward the rational, cognitive, critical approach to processing information. In spite of this, give my suggestions a try. It will bear fruit farther along, because one of our problems in approaching the scriptures is that we approach them in the cognitive, rational, critical mode. We stand off from them, look at them, evaluate them, and judge them in the light of who we are and our own agenda at that moment. We respond to the scriptures, but often our response is simply that of reading ourselves into the scriptures at some level rather than allowing God to speak to us out of them.

A third point I would like to suggest as we interact through this book is that you let your response take place down in the deeper levels of your being. Ask yourself questions such as: How do I feel about what is being said? How do I react? How do I respond down deep within? Then begin to ask yourself the questions: Why do I feel that way? Why am I responding in this manner? Why do I have these feelings within? What is going on down inside me? Let this exercise be an opportunity to get in touch with the deeper dynamics of your being. What do your reactions tell you about your habits, your attitudes, your perspectives, your responses and reactions to life? Are you beginning to see something about yourself? Thomas a Kempis said, "A humble knowledge of ourselves is a surer way to God than is the search for depth of learning."[2] That humble knowledge of yourself can come through a learning process if, as you read this book, you begin to balance your habitually cognitive, rational, intellectual response pattern by risking this affective dynamic of response deep within your being.

If you can do this while working through this book, it will begin to prepare you for spiritual reading. What I am trying to get you to do is begin to develop a mode of responding to informative material that will become formative. This mode of response will also help you begin to open up your "rational filter" by which, I believe, we filter out so much of God's voice. You will begin to hear at the heart and soul level. Jesus frequently reminded "those who had ears" to "hear,"[3] a strange exhortation unless it implies a hearing failure of some sort. My suspicion is that Jesus was talking about the operation of the "rational filter."

In our culture, we have been formed in such a way that we have ears to hear and do not hear. We don't know how to hear with the deeper levels of our being, and we need to rediscover this skill. If we are going to allow the scripture to become all that God intends for it to be in our spiritual formation, perhaps our biggest problem will be developing a mode of response to scripture that allows God to speak to us through it, clearly and transformingly, at these deeper levels of our being.

The three exercises I have suggested here may, through the course of this book, be a means of developing an alternate mode of response.

3.

The Nature of Spiritual Formation

C HRISTIAN spiritual formation is the process of being conformed to the image of Christ. In order to
have a common basis for our discussion throughout
this book, let us look briefly at the three elements of this
definition: Process, Being Conformed, Image of Christ.

PROCESS

Spiritual formation is not an instantaneous experience,
although there may well be instantaneous experiences at
certain points along the journey. This gradual aspect of
spiritual formation moves against the grain of our instant
gratification culture. We have been conditioned to expect
immediate returns on our investments. For this reason,
you may find it difficult, at points, to accept the necessity
of undergoing a lengthy period of spiritual discipline before experiencing any substantive change in your life. We
will touch upon this more deeply when we discuss spiritual disciplines.

Spiritual formation is not an option. Spiritual formation
is not a discipline just for "dedicated disciples." It is not a
pursuit only for the pious. Spiritual formation is not an ac-

tivity for the deeply committed alone. It is not a spiritual frill for those with the time and inclination. Spiritual formation is not a fad. *Spiritual formation is the primal reality of life.* Every unit of life is an experience of spiritual formation. Every action taken, every response made, every dynamic of relationship, every thought held, every emotion allowed: these are the miniscule arenas where, bit by bit, infinitesimal piece by infinitesimal piece, we are shaped into some kind of being. We are shaped either into the image of Christ or into a horribly destructive caricature.

Life is, by its very nature, spiritual formation. The question is not *whether* to undertake spiritual formation; the question is *what kind* of spiritual formation are we engaged in. Are we being increasingly conformed to the world, or are we being increasingly conformed to the image of Christ?

We will discover in the chapters which follow that one of the first dynamics of Christian spiritual formation is to come to grips with the negative and destructive spiritual formation that has been subtly ingrained into our being by our culture.

BEING CONFORMED

This aspect of spiritual formation also moves against the grain of our acculturation. Ours is an objectivizing, informational, functional culture. We are largely governed by a materialistic/humanistic world view which perceives everything "out there" as something to be grasped, controlled, and manipulated for our own purposes, or even for the purposes of God! This is so deeply ingrained, as we shall see, that we determine our own self-image, our meaning, our value, our purpose, by the effectiveness of our grasp, control, and manipulation of the world, other persons, even God. We seek to exercise our control by gaining information in order to manipulate what is "out there" for our purposes.

The very thought of "being conformed"—which clearly implies that we are to be grasped, controlled, and shaped by someone other than ourselves—militates against our deeply ingrained sense of being. "Graspers" powerfully resist being grasped by God. Controllers are inherently incapable of yielding control to God. Manipulators strongly reject being shaped by God. Information gatherers are structurally closed to being addressed by God. Information takers have extreme difficulty being receivers. Frenetically functional activists find it extremely difficult to "be still, and know" that God is God (Psalm 46:10, RSV). Already we see something of the deeper dynamics of what Jesus meant when he said, "Whoever would save his life [the grasping, controlling manipulator] will lose it; and whoever loses his life for my sake and the gospel's will save it" (Mark 8:35, RSV).

The expectation of instant gratification in our culture is a by-product of our grasping, controlling, manipulative way of living. It is a feedback we require to affirm for ourselves that we are effective persons. It confirms our functional self-identity. If what we do doesn't provide such gratification, it might mean that we are not capable, effective controllers of what is "out there." The idea of being conformed attacks these ingrained expectations. We have extreme difficulty in abiding, in waiting patiently, trustingly, perseveringly, for God to shape us according to his own agenda.

Genuine spiritual formation, being conformed, is the great reversal of the negative spiritual formation of our culture. It reverses our role from being the subject who controls the objects of the world, to being the object of the loving purposes of God who seeks to "control" us for our perfect wholeness. Genuine spiritual formation reverses our role as the controllers (who act to bring about the desired results in our lives), to beings who allow the spirit of God to act in our lives to bring about God's purposes. Genuine spiritual formation reverses our habitual expectations for gratification to a posture of patient, open-ended yielding. Genuine spiritual formation brings about a radical shift from being our own production to being God's workmanship.

THE IMAGE OF CHRIST

The goal of being conformed, the goal of the work which God seeks to accomplish in our lives, is that we should find our cleansing, healing, restoration, renewal, and transformation in an increasing likeness of our being and doing to that of Christ. Paul says it succinctly in Second Corinthians 3:17–18:

> Where the Spirit of the Lord is, there is freedom [from all that hinders our Christlikeness]. And we all, with unveiled face, beholding the glory of the Lord [the very essence of his being], are being transformed into his likeness from one degree of glory [our marred, misshapen image] to another [his perfect image].

This kind of spiritual formation takes place at the points of our unlikeness to the image of Christ. It is at precisely those points in our lives where we are not in conformity with the image of Christ that God encounters us. At those points God confronts us in our brokenness, challenges us to respond to his offer of forgiveness and healing, calls us to consecration of ourselves to him there; and, when we respond, God graciously works to conform us to the image of Christ at that point in our being.

The scripture stands close to the center of this whole process of being conformed to the image of Christ. As we shall see, the scripture is one of the primary channels through which God encounters us in our grasping, controlling, manipulative mode of existence. The scripture is one of the focal means whereby God awakens us to the dynamics and possibilities of a new way of being. We will now begin to consider how we can approach scripture so that it can become a transforming encounter with God.

II.

FOCAL PERCEPTUAL SHIFTS

Various Words of God

OUR PERCEPTUAL FRAMEWORKS

*W*E all have deeply ingrained perceptual frameworks that shape our lives in the world. Our perceptual framework consists of a complex structure of habit, attitude, perspective, relational dynamics, and response mechanisms. Our perceptual framework shapes our understanding of God, our understanding of ourselves, and our understanding of others. In the midst of living, our perceptual framework shapes our interaction in all three of these primal relationships of life. It conditions the way we respond and react to the situations of life.

These frameworks can, and most often do, become our prisons. We find ourselves in bondage to them. One of the roles of the scripture in spiritual formation is to liberate us from that bondage. Not only does scripture liberate us from the bondage of our perceptual framework, but at the same time it develops and nurtures within us a transformed and ever-expanding perceptual dynamic of wholeness wherein we find fullness of life in three primal relationships: with God, with self, with others.

Now the problem: How do we liberate the scripture from the bondage of the the old perceptual framework? There are four approaches to this problem that may help you come to some breakthroughs in your perceptual framework. First, I want to share with you some ideas on various words of God (this chapter). Second, I want to share some thoughts on information versus formation (chapter 5). Third, I want to share some insights on the iconographic nature of scripture (chapter 6). Finally, I want to share with you the biblical picture of "kairotic existence" (chapter 7).

YOU ARE A "WORD" OF GOD

Probably the necessary place to begin, whatever our perceptual framework, is with our understanding of ourselves. You are a "word" of God! Every human being is a word that God speaks into existence. Paul makes a profound statement in Ephesians 1:4: "Just as he [God] chose us in him [Christ] before the foundation of the world that we should be holy and blameless before him in love." I had read this passage for years, but suddenly I took notice of the word "chose." It is composed from two Greek words, the preposition *ek* and the basic word *lektos*, which comes from *lego*. *Ek* means "out of " or "forth from." *Lego* means "to speak." It seems perfectly legitimate to translate this compound word as "spoke forth." After all, if we "choose" someone or something, do we not speak them or it forth from among the other options we have? Thus Paul is saying that God "spoke us forth in Christ before the foundation of the world that we should be holy and blameless before him in love." It seems that Paul is taking us back to Genesis 1: "God said . . . and there was . . ." It takes us back to that primal Word of God by which all creation was "spoken forth" into being. But Paul takes us even further. He says that we are a word of God "spoken forth" *even before* the foundation of the world. There are tremendous implications here for our perception of human existence. Instead of human life being some type of derived result of either creation or evolution, Paul is implying that creation is subordinate to human existence!

Paul has a related insight in Romans 8:29, where he writes: "Those whom he foreknew he also predestined to be conformed to the image of his Son" (RSV). When Paul says, "those whom he foreknew," he is indicating that there was no emergency in heaven when you were conceived. There may have been a terrible emergency in your home! But your conception was no surprise to God. God purposed you into being. He spoke you forth from before the foundation of the world. God "foreknew" you into being.

Not only did God "speak you forth," but God spoke you forth into a very particular kind of shaping of that "word." God spoke us forth to be holy and blameless before him in love. "Holy" has to do with the wholeness of our being in the image of God; "blameless" has to do with our actions which flow out of that being. You see, God is involved with both the being and doing dynamics of our lives. Paul expresses this in another way in the passage in Romans: "Those whom he foreknew he also predestined to be conformed to the image of his Son." Being holy and blameless is the same as being conformed to the image of Jesus in our being and our doing.

The heart of the matter is that God has spoken us forth. Some saint has said, "You are the breath of God, and God is right now breathing you."[1] There is something in us that touches God. This takes us back to Genesis 2, where it says God formed humanity from the dust of the earth and breathed into them the breath of life and they became living beings. After the "word" image of Genesis 1, we find the "breath" image of Genesis 2. God breathes us forth into being. So we are, in some sense, God's "breath." The "word" which God is breathing us forth to be is his will for our wholeness in Christ's image.

THE INCARNATION OF OUR "WORD"

Now our "word," this word with a small "w" that God is breathing forth, is incarnate in us. Our physical life; our psychological, mental, emotional life—our whole created being is the vehicle for the expression of that "word" God speaks us forth to be in the lives of others. We are incarnate "words" of God. Our attitudes, our behaviors show forth the "word" we are. In all that we are and in all that we do with one another in the world, God is seeking to bring to full expression that "word" spoken forth by God.

But the "word" we are, this "word" incarnate in us, is constantly being shaped in us—in our incarnation. It is being shaped either positively or negatively—positively when our "word" is being shaped by the Word of God, negatively when our "word" is being garbled and distorted and debased by the values and structures of the world. The fact is, our "word" *has* becomed garbled by the intrusion of false and incomplete expressions of being. Our "word" *has* become distorted by the infiltration of damaging and destructive dynamics of life. Our "word" *has* become debased by the invasion of manipulative models of relationship. Probably one of the reasons you are reading this book is that you want to move forward on your pilgrimage, your quest, your search, your journey. Perhaps you are seeking to allow your "word" to become more clearly the "word" that God speaks you forth to be in the world and in the lives of others. Perhaps you wish to learn how the garblings, distortions, and debasings of your "word" can be cleansed and healed and that word clearly spoken forth in you life.

The problem is that there are manifold dynamics of this debasing of the "word" God speaks us forth to be. In our deep inner habits, in our ingrained attitudes and hardened perspectives, in our predictable outer reactions and fixed responses, we debase that "word" God speaks us forth to be. This, in large measure, is what Paul was wrestling with in Romans 7. There is a great debate among scholars as to whether Romans 7 describes the pre-Christian Paul or the post-conversion Christian Paul. I am convinced from my own experience (and that of others in Christian history) that it must have been post-conversion Paul. I experience what Paul talked about, and I am sure you do too. Paul said, "The good I want to do I don't do and the evil I don't want to do is what I do" (Rom. 7:19). Paul, like us, found that there were dynamics of being within him that were inconsistent with God's will for his wholeness. He found that the "word" God spoke him forth to be was garbled, distorted, and debased. Even after coming to know Jesus in a personal way, we too discover this reality. This discovery usually puts us on a spiritual quest. We begin to realize we need far more wholeness, far more healing, far more cleansing than what we have experienced if we are to become the "word" God speaks us forth to be in the world.

The Living, Penetrating, Transforming Word of God

The focal shaping of our "word" into wholeness comes by allowing our "word" to be shaped by the Word of God. There is some profound sense in which our "word" is hidden in the Word. The essential dynamics of our "word" are found in the Word of God. When we begin to allow our "word" to echo to the Word, we begin to experience increasing levels of wholeness in our being. We begin to experience that quality of wholeness in our interactions with others and our involvement in life for which we were spoken forth by God. I hope this begins to put scripture, which we speak of as the Word of God, into a somewhat different dimension for you. I hope you are beginning to experience some transformation of your perceptual framework.

Now, what is the Word by which we are to be shaped? Let me combine two members of the Trinity and speak of Jesus as the Word and the Spirit also as the Word, the two primary modes in which we see the Word of God in scripture. Jesus as the Word is set forth most clearly in the prologue of John's Gospel: "In the beginning was the Word, and the Word was with God, and the Word was God. . . . And the Word became flesh" (John 1:1, 14, RSV).

Another place where we see Jesus clearly depicted as the Word is in Revelation 19. Jesus is seen as the One riding on the great white horse, and one of the names by which he is called is "the Word of God." In this depiction of Jesus as the Word of God, there is also the image of the sharp two-edged sword coming out of his mouth. This image is earlier introduced in Revelation 1 and 2, where Jesus is the One having the sharp two-edged sword going forth from his mouth. The picture of the two-edged sword recalls Ephesians 6, where Paul speaks of the sword of the Spirit which is the Word of God. Through these images in early Christian perception, both Jesus and the Spirit are seen as two polarities of one reality: the Word of God.

This Word of God, present in Jesus and active in the Holy Spirit, has at least two dimensions. First, it is the context of all that is. This is what is being conveyed in the prologue of John's Gospel. The Word is the source, the sustenance, the formative dynamic of all that is. Nothing was made without the Word. Everything comes into being through the Word, is sustained by the Word, and has life in the Word. This means that even our "word" that is spoken forth from God is spoken forth within the context of the Word.

Second, the Word became flesh. This Word is a Word that is involved in human existence. It is not some sort of static concept. In New Testament times, Stoic philosophy, the prevailing philosophy of the age, had a concept of *logos* or "word." "Word" was that shaping, organizing, forming principle of the universe which held everything together and directed its course; but it was a very impersonal, uninvolved kind of word. The Word we are speaking of is a Word that is actively involved in human existence. Here is one of those dimensions of the incarnation so important for us to grasp: not simply the idea of God becoming human (not that we should lose that) but that the Word of God is intimately and vitally involved with us in the midst of life. The Word continues to come to his own, many of whom continue to receive him not; but to those who receive the Word, he still gives power to become children of God—the children God speaks them forth to be in the world.

Perhaps the writer of Hebrews caught it best in Hebrews 4:12–13. "The Word of God is living and productive"; that is, it is an active and creative presence in our lives, seeking to bring forth the purposes of God. Then the writer uses the same two-edged sword image we have seen before, "sharper than any two-edged sword, cutting to the divi-

VARIOUS WORDS OF GOD

sion of soul and spirit, of joints and marrow." "Joints and marrow" is an adequate translation, but it does not really get to the roots of the Greek words; *joints* and *marrow* are secondary meanings of the terms. The word for *joint* is, in its essential meaning, that which unites things, the bonding dynamic which holds the parts of something in proper relationship. The word for *marrow,* in its essential meaning, is that which is at the heart or essence of something. What the writer of Hebrews is saying then is that the Word of God goes to the very center of what we are. It cuts through to that which bonds us together as a being, it touches upon that which forms the essence of what we are. Then, just in case we missed the point, the writer continues, with "discerning the thoughts and intentions of the heart."

The writer of Hebrews goes on in a very interesting phrase: "No creation is hidden from him." We are not dealing here with an optional dynamic of human life. The Word of God is an intimate and vital presence in all human life. Again, I suspect that you are reading this book because you have begun to realize that the living, productive Word of God is not an optional presence in your life. You have begun to realize that same Word interpenetrating your life in some way. You have come to the point in your spiritual pilgrimage where you realize your wholeness depends upon your response to that Word, and you are seeking a deeper and fuller response.

Then, in an even more interesting phrase, the writer adds, "But all are naked and laid bare before his eyes." Here again the original Greek conveys a much more dynamic image. The word "laid bare" is a word that comes both from gladiatorial combat in the arena and from the sacrificial altar. In association with the altar, it describes the position of the sacrifice with its head pulled back and its throat exposed for the sacrificial knife. In association with gladiatorial combat, it describes the position of the vanquished gladiator as he is laid across the knee of the victor with his throat exposed for the death blow of the knife. The writer of Hebrews is saying this is our posture before the Word of God—a position of total, absolute, unconditional vulnerability! If this doesn't make you uncomfortable, just imagine yourself naked and laid back exposed as a gladiator or sacrificial animal would have been. It gives you some perception of total vulnerability. This is the posture we have before that living, productive, penetrating Word of God.

The writer of Hebrews closes with his most profound affirmation about the Word of God. He writes that we are totally vulnerable "before the eyes of him with respect to whom the Word is for us." In spite of the fact that the imagery of the Word's encounter with us is filled with pictures of painful penetration, in spite of the imagery of the Word of God which cuts through to the very center of our life, in spite of the imagery of the Word which deals with us discerningly (and, therefore, disruptively?) at the deep levels of our being, in spite of the image of our total, absolute vulnerability before the two-edged sword of the living Word, in spite of all these disturbing and painful images, the writer affirms that the Word is *for* us! It is for our wholeness. It is for our re-creation. It is for our transformation, not our destruction. Only those elements of our being which are inconsistent with God's will for our wholeness will be destroyed. These, of course, must go. If we submit to the scalpel of a skilled surgeon, we trust him or her to cut to the core of the problem and to remove from our bodies whatever is inconsistent with physical wholeness. There is a profound sense in which the Word of God is a living and productive scalpel in the loving hands of One who penetrates to the core of our being to cleanse and heal our garbled, distorted, debased word and transform it into the word God speaks us forth to be in the world.

THE INTRUSIVE WORD OF GOD

The Word is truly the mediator between us and God. The Word is "for us" with respect to God, and it is also "for God" with respect to us. This introduces the intrusive nature of the Word of God. The Word of God breaks into the midst of life. Merton speaks of the Word of God meeting us in encounter and event.[2]

Let me give you my definition of the Word of God: the

Word of God is the action of the presence, the purpose, and the power of God in the midst of human life. Now this is a very broad, general definition. There are many specifics which can be placed within this general definition: the Old Testament accounts of the presence, power, and purpose of God in the history of Israel and the lives of various individuals; the presence, power, and purpose of God most fully revealed in the life, death, resurrection, and ascension of Jesus; the New Testament accounts of the presence, power, and purpose of God through the Holy Spirit in the life of the early church and various individuals; and the presence, power, and purpose of God in the post-biblical history of the church. While we tend to think of scripture as the Word of God, and unquestionably the action of the presence, power, and purpose of God in human existence is experienced most fully in scripture, scripture is a distillation of the action of the Word of God which is diffused through all of human life and activity.

What I am trying to do is to help you develop a context in which to view the scripture which, perhaps, will help you approach the scripture with a new perceptual framework. For example, take the topic of "spiritual reading." We tend to think of spiritual reading as reading the scripture first of all, and this is sound. But if you have some acquaintance with Christian literature, you know the writings of the great masters of Christian spirituality can become sources for spiritual reading. Poems, novels, plays can also become spiritual reading because all of these human vehicles can become channels for the action of God's presence, purpose, and power to penetrate our own lives. The secret is that spiritual reading has more to do with approach than with the content. Even the scripture, if approached without any openness to encounter with God, may be dead and lifeless; whereas hungry, seeking hearts have been ushered into the presence, power, and purpose of God while meditating on some piece of secular literature.

SCRIPTURE AS THE WORD OF GOD

Let me now focus upon the scripture as the Word of God, and try to bring together what we have been considering. First of all, the scripture is the optimum record of the intrusion of the Word of God into human history. It is the record of that focal event, or a whole sequence of focal events, wherein the Word of God has broken into human lives. It is the picture of human encounter with the action of the presence, purpose, and power of God in the midst of human situations. As such, scripture provides insight into the ways in which the Word penetrates human lives and situations, discerns/reveals the truth of the human condition, and transforms the garbled, distorted, debased words human beings have become into the words God speaks them forth to be in the world.

Second, not only is scripture a record of the intrusion of the living, productive Word of God, it is also a revelation of the Word as the matrix or context of both human brokenness and human wholeness. As such a revelation, the Word of God is portrayed in scripture as doing at least three things. (1) When that Word of God intrudes, encounters, or breaks in, it addresses human beings in their brokenness. That is part of the Good News: we don't have to measure up to some level of wholeness before the Word addresses us. (2) The Word calls us to wholeness right at the point of our brokenness! We are addressed and called at the same time. In Revelation 3:19, Jesus says, "Those whom I love I reprove and nurture." Here God's encounter with human brokenness and God's offer of nurture into wholeness are conjoined. The scripture is a revelation of the Word addressing our brokenness and calling us to wholeness. (3) Scripture is the revelation of the Word as the agent of transformation.

Perhaps a look at Second Timothy 3:16–17, will help to clarify these dynamics. Paul begins with a very puzzling phrase. If different translations are read we find, "All scripture is inspired by God," (RSV), "All God-inspired scripture,"[3] "Every inspired scripture" (NEB), and a number of other phrasings. Something we usually fail to recognize in our working with the scripture, and particularly with the letters of Paul, is the Hebrew love of pun. The Hebrews used puns for conveying multiple layers of meanings, utilizing terms which would resonate with more than one level of meaning at the same time.

I suspect that Paul is using a pun at the beginning of Second Timothy 3:16. What is involved here is what I like to think of as the dynamic inspiration of the scripture. Not only is there the dynamic of God's inspiration in the writing of the scripture, there is also the dynamic of God's inspiration in our reading of the scripture. The Word of God which encountered the writer and of which he wrote also addresses us. Wesley was sensitive to this aspect of scripture when he instructed the early Methodists, "Serious and earnest prayer should be constantly used before we consult the oracles of God; seeing 'Scripture can only be understood through the same Spirit whereby it was given.'"[4] When we are open to God on our side of the inspirational equation, the creative inspiration of the scripture becomes the productive inspiration of God in our lives. We become an inherent part of the inspiration of the scriptures.

The problem today is that there tends to be a polarity here. More conservative Christians tend to think of the Bible as the inspired Word of God, with all inspiration relating to its writing. Less conservative Christians tend to think of inspiration as something that happens to the individual reader. They claim that a person can be inspired by the Bible or can be equally inspired by the Bhagavad-gita or the Koran or anything else. In the Christian tradition, however, there is a unique conjoining of both halves of the inspirational dynamic. God's inspiration of the writer and God's inspiration of the reader are two halves of a whole, and to lose *either half* is to erect in our hearing of the scripture a filter that will block out a tremendous amount of the living, penetrating, transforming Word of God. We might end up doing one of two things: slavishly worshipping the Bible or standing back and critically assessing and picking from among the biblical tidbits those which seem to "inspire" us. Either extreme is deadly and deadening to spiritual wholeness. There needs to be the vital conjoining of both halves of the inspirational equation.

Such a conjoining is what Paul was doing when he employed the phrase "all 'God-breathed' scripture" in Second Timothy 3:16. His pun indicates the possibility of a dual "God-breathing"—the breathing of God which brought the scripture into being and what God is breathing you forth to be as you read it. The Spirit of God at work in our lives brings us into companionship with the text in such a way that the Word of God begins to shape the word which God speaks us forth to be in the world. When we begin to come to the scripture in this perspective, there is an openness for us to be addressed by the Word incarnated in what we call the scripture.

When the scripture becomes inspired in this dynamic, dual mode, when it becomes truly the encounter with the living, productive, penetrating Word of God, then, Paul tells us, four things happen. First, the encounter with the living Word is profitable for teaching. There is a very clear distinction made by Paul and the other New Testament writers between "teaching" (in the singular) and "teachings" (in the plural). The plural form is used in the New Testament always in conjunction with the activities of either human beings or demons.[5] The singular form always has to do with the proclamation of the Good News of what God has done and is doing through Jesus Christ. Thus the encounter with the living Word of God is the intrusion of the reality of the new life in Christ into our life. The possibility of a radically new mode of being is revealed to us.

Second, the "God-breathed" scripture is profitable for reproof. Here we see that encounter with the living Word which penetrates to the deep center of our being, discerns the thoughts and intentions of our hearts, and addresses us at the points of our brokenness. The scripture brings into sharp relief the garbled, distorted, debased nature of the word we have become. We begin to see the distinction between what we are and what God is speaking us forth to be.

Third, the inspired scripture is profitable for correction. The Greek original is not really captured by the word "correction." The Greek term means to bring something into straightness or into alignment or to bring something into wholeness. Here we begin to see the way in which the Word is "for us." Not only does the living Word present us with the possibility of a whole new mode of being, not only does it bring to light those things in us which are inconsistent with that mode of being, but it provides us the opportunity of obedience as the channel through which God brings our lives into the wholeness of that new mode of being in Christ.

Fourth, Paul says "God-breathed" scripture is profitable for training in righteousness. That word "training" is a loaded term in the Greek. It is the word *paideia,* from which we get "pedagogy." *Paideia* was that complex process in the Hellenistic culture of the New Testament world by which an infant was nurtured, educated, trained, disciplined, guided, and instructed. Thus the child was brought from infancy to full, mature, participating membership in the *polis* (the Greek term for "city" which was the entire social, economic, political, religious, and cultural matrix which gave meaning, purpose, and value to human existence). Paul and the other New Testament writers take over this term to speak of the work of God in the life of God's people. Earlier we saw that the living Word of God addresses our brokenness, calls us to wholeness, and is the agent of transformation. Paul is speaking here of this last activity of the Word. This is the steady, consistent, daily nurturing of our lives by the Word so that we are increasingly shaped by the Word in the inner dynamics of our being.

Paul concludes his description of the role of the living, productive Word of God in our lives by indicating the purpose of this shaping: "In order that the person of God might be complete" (2 Tim. 3:17). The Greek word here is a beautiful one. It is the word *artios,* meaning that which is perfectly suited to its nature. If you went to a fruit bowl and found what you considered to be a perfect apple, you would call it *artios.* It would be everything an apple ought to be. This is the term Paul uses for the goal of our being shaped by the Word. The purpose of this shaping by the living Word is to nurture us into being all God speaks us forth to be. But Paul indicates that the goal of our shaping by the Word is not only that we might be perfectly suited to our nature, but "that God's person might be equipped for every good work" (2 Tim. 3:17). What Paul is saying is that when our word is shaped by the Word in our inner being, our life in the world will be shaped according to that same Word. Our word will become the word God speaks us forth to be *in the lives of others*. Increasingly we will become God's, spoken forth into the life of the world.

We have been considering various words of God, attempting to expand our perceptual framework by realizing that we are each a "word" that God is speaking forth into the world. God is speaking us forth, especially, to be his in the lives of others. We have also been trying to expand our perception of the scripture as the Word of God by sketching the outline of the role of the Word in the shaping of that "word" God speaks us forth to be.

I hope you have been open to God as you read this chapter. What have you been feeling? How have you reacted to the ideas presented? Why have you responded as you did? Does your response reveal anything about yourself? About your relationship with God? Has God been addressing you at any point? Has your perceptual framework been changed in any way? How? Why? What is your perception of who you are in relationship with God? What is your understanding of the scripture as the Word of God?

Perhaps you need to take time to meditate upon these questions before moving on to the next stage of reordering your perceptual framework: Information Verses Formation.

5.

Information Versus Formation

---

*W*ILL you begin this chapter by opening yourself to the Lord in prayer, seeking the fullness of the work of God's purposes in your life? You might want to join me in prayer:

> *O God, We rejoice that this time we share together in this chapter is set within the deeper context of your presence, your purpose, and your power. We want to open ourselves to whatever it is you want to do with us. Open us up at the deeper levels of our beings that we might be aware of the touches of your grace upon our lives, that we may be responsive and receptive to whatever it is you want to do. Amen.*

As we developed the first point—the perception of our being a word spoken forth by God into the world and the shaping of our word by the Word of God—it probably became clear to you that we need a new perspective for our approach to scripture in the process of spiritual formation. The second point I want to share with you regarding the transformation of our perceptual framework is the contrast between the *informational* and the *formational* approach to scripture.

47

THE INFORMATIONAL-FUNCTIONAL CULTURE

In a chapter of *Asking the Fathers* entitled "Holy Reading," Aelred Squire quotes William of St. Thierry:

> The Scriptures need to be read in the same spirit in which they were written, and only in that spirit are they to be understood. You will never reach an understanding of Paul until, by close attention to reading him and the application of continual reflection, you imbibe his spirit. You will never arrive at understanding David until by the actual experience you realize what the psalms are about. And so it is with the rest. In every piece of Scripture, real attention is as different from mere reading as friendship is from entertainment, or the love of a friend from a casual greeting.

Squire then adds:

> Taken seriously, how devastating a criticism such a passage is of many of our modern habits of reading, and even of much that passes for study, with its clattering and noisy apparatus and comparative indifference to real content. If, in our own day, we are to do 'holy reading' in the traditional sense of that phrase, nothing but conscious choice and the development of conscious habits of attention will be likely to cure us of a dissipation of mind that so much that we see and hear is designed to foster. As William of St. Thierry goes on to point out, it is less what one reads than *how* one reads that counts. It is an attitude of mind that is at issue.[1]

This is precisely the point of difference between the informational and formational approach to material. We are a culture shaped by the informational mode. This informational mode is an integral part of what I call the "functional" orientation of our culture. Ours is a culture which seeks more information (new facts, new bodies of knowledge, new techniques, new methods, new systems, new programs) in order to improve its functional control of its environment. The acquiring of knowledge, information, techniques, methods, and systems, rather than serving to change the quality of our being, is for the primary purpose of improving or enhancing our ability to function so as to change the world to our parameters. Thus the informational mode of our culture is a companion piece with the functional mode.

These informational-functional dynamics are so deeply ingrained in the whole fabric of our culture that they have become one of those binding and/or blinding perceptions which take over automatically whenever we open a book. We have been trained to seek only information when it comes to reading.

THE NATURE OF INFORMATIONAL READING

Here are some of the characteristics of informational reading. First, informational reading seeks to cover as much as possible as quickly as possible. Isn't it interesting that the profusion of speed reading techniques has arisen at the same time our culture has become increasingly informational in its technological functionalism? One of the adverse aspects of this approach is seen in programs designed to read the entire Bible in a brief period of time.

Second, informational reading is linear. We move from the first element to the second to the third and on to the end, thinking that reading is little more than the process of movement through the parts.

Let me give you an example of this dynamic in bibilical interpretation. Most interpreters of Revelation do not realize that the events of chapters 17–22 are intended to be seen as three facets of a single profound vision. Most commentators presume that 17:1–19:10, the vision of the Harlot of the Beast (Fallen Babylon), precedes the vision of the great judgment of God in Christ in 19:11–21:8, which, in turn, precedes the vision of the Bride of the Lamb (New Jerusalem) in 21:9–22:10. The introductory elements to the visions of the two women (17:1–3, 21:9–10) and the concluding elements (19:9–10, 22:6–10) reveal that these two visions are to be understood as parallel pieces, joined in some way by the vision of the judgment. It is John's falling down to worship the angel a second time (22:8), after he had been previously ordered not to do it (19:10), which provides the clue to understanding this final complex of visions in Revelation. The repetition of John's worship of the angel is not a repetition—*it is the same event!*

John's vision is a holistic revelation of the profound consequences of God's judgment in Jesus Christ. In the judgment of God in Christ, Fallen Babylon, the whole order of rebellion against God, is disestablished; New Jerusalem, the new order of being in Christ, is eternally established. There is much more here, but this serves to illustrate how linear reading misses the deeper dimensions of a passage.

Third, in informational reading we seek to master the text. We seek to grasp it, to get our minds around it, to bring it under *our* control. Having done this, we then seek to justify our control (interpretation) and defend it against any other controls (interpretations).

Fourth, a characteristic of informational reading is that the text is an object "out there" for us to control and/or manipulate according to our own purposes, intentions, or desires. We back off and keep ourselves at a distance from the text. This is a focal part of that informational mode which so pervades our whole learning process and our whole perceptual framework.

Fifth, this approach to reading is analytical, critical, and judgmental. This is the outgrowth of standing back and running what we read through the filters of our own perceptions, our own desires, our own wants, our own needs. Here we see the application of the cognitive, rational, intellectual approach we noted in chapter 2. Don't misunderstand me. I am not saying that informational reading is wrong in and of itself. It has its place, as we shall see in a moment; but its place is somewhat less primary than what our cultural perceptions have ingrained in us.

Sixth, informational reading is characterized by a problem-solving mentality. This feeds back to the functional mode of existence. We tend to read in order to find out something that will work for us, whether it is to read the instruction manual on a piece of equipment that isn't working the way it should, or to read some spiritual instruction manual so we can make some changes in our spiritual life at points where it is not "working properly."

We have a strong tendency to approach our reading tasks informationally. This approach to reading is really an unconscious activity. You probably had never even thought of it until this book brought it to your attention; it is unconscious with us; it is deeply ingrained within us. You may be racing through this book with the old, informational dynamics; covering it as quickly as possible, seeking to master the text, to bring it under your control, to analyze it to see if it fits your agenda, and to determine whether you can "use" it to do what you want in your spiritual life. If this is the case, where is there a space, a silence, in which God can speak? Where can the Word address the word you are? The informational mode of reading tends to maintain those dynamics of the old perceptual framework which garble and distort and debase the word God speaks us forth to be in the world.

THE INFORMATIONAL MODE IN READING THE BIBLE

Thomas Merton picks up several significant consequences of the informational mode for our reading of the scripture: "In order to read the Bible honestly, we have to avoid entrenching ourselves behind official positions, whether religious or cultural, whether for or against the Bible itself."[2] That kind of entrenchment, no matter what it is, is of the informational mode. From within our entrenched position, we seek to read the Bible to find more support for our position or to explain away anything which seems not to fit our position. This is the analytical, problem-solving dynamic of the informational mode. The text is an object to be controlled and manipulated. The text is something "out there" which *we* control, and the basis of our control is that entrenched position we bring to the text. It doesn't make any difference, as Merton said, whether it is a religious presupposition or a cultural one; the text remains an object of our manipulation.

Again Merton writes (and this one may pinch a bit),

"Curiously, the most serious religious people, or the most concerned scholars, [he could have left that one out!] those who constantly read the Bible as a matter of professional or pious duty, can often manage to evade a radically involved dialogue with the book they are questioning."[3]

As we will see, this is primarily because we tend to use the informational approach, particularly as students of the Bible. We often are not looking for a "radically involved dialogue." We are more often seeking some tidbits of information that will enhance our understanding of the Christian faith without challenging or confronting the way we live in the world. As Merton points out:

> Good Biblical scholarship is essential for a serious understanding of the Bible, but this scientific itch for arid and pointless investigations which throw no new light on anything whatever has deadened our sensitivity to the existential reality of Biblical experience. . . . We shall always find in it as much as we seek and no more.[4]

Then Merton begins to provide the corrective for a basically informational approach to the scripture, "Any serious reading of the Bible means personal involvement in it, not simply mental agreement with abstract propositions. And involvement is dangerous, because it lays one open to unforseen conclusions."[5] In the informational approach to reading we give assent, mental agreement, to abstract conceptualizations; but we do not, at least in informational reading, tend to involve ourselves personally, intimately, openly, receptively in that which we read. It is too dangerous for us, too threatening.

Finally, Merton writes:

> To accept the Bible in its *wholeness* is not easy. We are much more inclined to narrow it down to a one-track interpretation which actually embraces only a very limited aspect of it. And we dignify that one-track view with the term "faith". . . . All attempts to narrow the Bible down until it fits conveniently into the slots prepared for it by our preju-

dice will end with our misunderstanding the Bible and even falsifying its truth.[6]

Here again, Merton is talking about the consequence of the informational approach in which the scripture becomes an object of our attention and control.

THE NATURE OF FORMATIONAL READING

Now let us look at the alternative. I suspect that from what I have said about the informational approach to reading, you already have some perception that the formational approach is a radical alternative to our normal posture of being with regard to reading and study. Let me share some of the balancing characteristics of reading for formation versus reading for information.

First, in contrast to reading for information, the object is not to cover as much as possible as quickly as possible; reading for formation avoids quantifying the amount of reading in any sort of way. You are not concerned at all with the amount. You are concerned with small portions. You may find yourself "holding" on just one sentence or one paragraph or perhaps as much as a whole page, but probably not more than that. You are not concerned with getting through the book. So what if it takes you a year, two years, five years to get through the book? That is not the point.

Perhaps there are some things grating inside you right now. You may be saying, "That's not *reading!* I've got this book; I've got to get through it." Do you ever find yourself thumbing through a book to see how many pages are left in the chapter you are reading? This may be a symptom of informational reading. Or, hopefully, you find yourself stopping and going back and reflecting, perhaps dropping back a paragraph or maybe even a whole chapter and saying, "Hey, I missed something here. There are deeper levels of meaning here, and I have to slow down and meditate on them." This is an indication that you may have begun to move into formational reading.

Second, although informational reading is linear, trying

to move quickly over the surface of the text, formational reading is in depth. You are seeking to allow the passage to open out to you its deeper dynamics, its multiple layers of meaning. Instead of rushing on to the next sentence, paragraph, or chapter, you seek to move deeper and deeper and deeper into the text. In reading the Bible, for example, you seek to allow the text to begin to become that intrusion of the Word of God into your life, to address you, to encounter you. If you don't take time with a text, the Word cannot encounter you in it; the Word of God cannot speak to you through it.

What happens in personal relationships if, as you see someone coming toward you, you start walking toward them talking steadily as you approach, come up to them, shake the person's hand, and continue on, talking the whole time? Has there been any address from them? This is just what we tend to do with reading material. We pick up the book and our minds immediately start informing that text. We go all the way through the text telling it what we want it to say to us. When we finish we say, "That was a great book" or "That was a lousy book." The book has never really had a chance to address us.

Third, in informational reading we seek to grasp the control, to master the text. I suspect you already see what the third point is in formational reading: it is to allow the text to master you. In reading the Bible, this means we come to the text with an openness to hear, to receive, to respond, to be a servant of the Word rather than a master of the text.

Fourth, instead of the text being an object we control and manipulate according to our own insight and purposes, the text becomes the subject of the reading relationship; we are the object that is shaped by the text. With respect to biblical reading, we willingly stand ourselves before the text and await its address, ready for the Word to exercise control over the word we are. This is one of the reasons why formational reading cannot be quantified. It requires waiting before the text. You have to take time with it in order to hear what it says.

Let me share with you a personal experience along this line. I had been using a lectionary for directing my spiritual reading in the Bible. The Old Testament portion was taking me through the Exodus event, and I was reading the section about the contest, the struggle, between God and Pharaoh portrayed in the series of plagues. Now, I have read that portion of the Old Testament countless times. I have studied it in detail on several occasions; but, unfortunately, I apparently had been reading it informationally all the time.

During this period of reading, however, I would read the daily portion assigned by the lectionary and then I would sit before it and say, "Lord, what are you seeking to say to me through this? What is your Word of address to me?" All sorts of thoughts would be going through my mind— Moses said this and Pharaoh did that, Pharaoh's resistance, God's hardening of Pharaoh's heart—all thoughts I had been through many, many times. I knew everything that was there, and I really seemed to be getting nothing from it. There seemed to be no "Word from the Lord." However, one important (but uncomfortable) thing about a lectionary is that if you make it a spiritual discipline, you cannot move beyond it. You can't just move on and get to the "good parts" or the sections which appeal to you or seem to speak to you. You have to stay with the portion assigned. Well, I had been wrestling with this portion of Exodus for a week or more. Each day the lectionary moved me to a new portion of the plagues, sort of a "plague a day." Each day I would stop and ask, "Lord, what are you seeking to say to me in this passage?" Each day I was met with silence—or the noise of my own understanding of the passage.

One morning, as the lectionary moved me toward the end of the plagues, I read the portion and then asked the same question I had asked each day, "Lord, what are you seeking to say to me here?" This time the answer came.

"You are Pharaoh!"

"What?" I replied. "Me, Pharaoh? Moses perhaps, even one of the Hebrew people, but *Pharaoh?* Perhaps one of the servants, one of the slaves, perhaps a taskmaster, Lord?"

"You are Pharaoh!"

Then, with that Word, things began to open up—in the text and in me. I began to realize that, as a word spoken forth by God, God had spoken certain qualities into my "word." God had given me certain gifts and abilities and characteristics, certain qualities of personality. God had also shaped my "word" by being an active presence in the various experiences of my life. All of these dynamics of my "word" were God's "children," but I had enslaved them to my own purposes, my own desires, my own intentions, my own plans. Truly I *was* Pharaoh in my life!

As I began to wrestle with this Word, the lectionary brought me to the final plague, the death of the firstborn. I began to realize that for me to cease to be Pharaoh in my life, there would have to be the death of my "firstborn" desires to use God's gifts for my own purposes. If those gifts were to be liberated for God's use in my life and ministry, if they were to be the "word" God was speaking me forth to be in the world, I would have to cease to be Pharaoh.

This is what can happen when we come to the text formationally rather than informationally, when we allow the Word to address us through the text, when we are willing to take the posture of the object which the text addresses rather than trying to control it.

Fifth, instead of the analytical, critical, judgmental approach of informational reading, formational reading requires a humble, detached, willing, loving approach. This is a rather tall order because it requires a radical reorientation of the inner posture of our being. We can slow down the pace of our reading. We can probe more deeply into the text. We can even begin to view the text as addressing us, without any radical shift of our perceptions or our inner posture of being. We simply make some adjustments to our informational mode. However, when we come to genuine openness and receptivity to the Word, to yieldedness to the penetrating address of God which confronts our garbled, distorted, debased word, to a willing pliability before the sharp sword of the Word, then we come up against the need for something more than simple adjustments to the status quo. Here we begin to hear the call to spiritual disciplines of a deeper order.

Sixth, a characteristic of informational reading is the problem-solving mentality. In contrast, a characteristic of formational reading is openness to mystery. Instead of the problem-solving mentality, instead of coming to what we are reading to find a solution for something else in our life, we come to be open to that Mystery we call *God*. We come to stand before that Mystery and to allow that Mystery to address us. Eventually, we may discover that tremendous problem-solving dynamics emerge out of that encounter. But here is the difficult part: we don't enter into the encounter to get problem-solving results. This is where a major part of the relinquishment in formational reading comes in.

You will discover that you really have to guard against yourself at this point. We are such subtle beings that we can let the old, problem-solving, self-oriented mentality slip in the back door or the side window unnoticed when we have closed and barred the front door to it. Again and again you will find yourself slipping back into the informational mode of reading at this point because the informational mode is very protective. When the Word begins to address us, one of our first tendencies (presuming we are operating in the formational mode) is to slip back into the informational mode. To slip back to the informational mode reverses the roles—you again are the "master," and the text again becomes the "object" which you can control, thus limiting its influence upon your life. You will find it a strong temptation to slip back into the informational mode at these points, especially if the Word which addresses you penetrates your life at a particularly painful point in your spiritual condition.

As you can see, this formational approach to the use of scripture is a discipline which needs to be developed. Preparation is necessary for formational reading. With informational reading you can run in, sit down, pick up the book, and go at it. It doesn't require any prior preparation. Formational reading, however, requires time to "center down," to use the old Quaker phrase, to become still, to relinquish, to let go of your life in the presence of God.

We tend to race through our lives frantically maintaining a precarious control on our fast-moving vehicle of life. We need time to slow down. We need time to let go of the controls. We need time to relax in order to be prepared in our inner spirits for formational reading. Even this preparation itself is spiritually forming. I hope you can see that just coming to the point where you can open the text formationally is already a tremendous spiritual formation. Even if no Word addresses you out of that text on that day, or that week, or that month, the constant discipline of preparing yourself and entering into formational reading will itself be spiritually forming.

INFORMATIONAL-FORMATIONAL INTERPLAY AND BALANCE

What we discover in the use of scripture in spiritual formation is that it is not the method that is the most important thing. We have not yet come to the point where we can begin to think about methods. Instead of methods, it is our *motive* that is primary. Our approach to the scripture will be shaped by our motive. We tend to think of informational and formational as two different techniques for reading. The real issue is not a matter of which technique is best or even what is the optimum combination of techniques, but rather what posture toward the mystery of God can open us up to formational possibilities. If we come to the informational aspect of reading with this inner posture of openness to God, the informational task will then lead us to the formative dynamic.

You may have inferred from what I have said so far that the informational mode is of the "dark realm" or something like that. I do not mean to imply that at all. I have been overstressing the alternative to informational reading in order to highlight the contrast for you. Merton has a very good synopsis of the interplay between the informational and formational modes. He writes, "This [engagement with the biblical text], as Bultmann has shown, requires two levels of understanding: first, a preliminary unravelling of the meaning of the texts themselves, a *Vorver-ständnis*, which is mainly a matter of knowledge acquired by study."[7] This is the informational dynamic, and Merton is correct in saying it is important. But there is, he continues:

> a deeper level, a living insight which grows out of personal involvement and relatedness: *Lebensverhältnis*. Only on this second level is the Bible really grasped, and it is to this deeper level . . . that the writers and editors of the Biblical canon obviously addressed themselves.[8]

There must be this constant interplay between the informational and formational modes of reading. But Merton has it straight; the informational mode is only the "front porch" of the role of scripture in spiritual formation. It is, you might say, the point of entry into the text. But once we have crossed the porch, we must enter into that deeper encounter with the Word which is the formational approach.

There is a need for balance here. You may start with the informational dynamics, but you must be sensitive to the need to move to the formational dynamics of reading. You must allow yourself to become open and receptive to the intrusion of the living Word of God into the garbled, distorted, and debased "word" you are. You must be responsive to the word God is speaking you forth to be in the world. You may start with the formational dynamics but frequently find that you get tripped up on an informational point. You will need to back off momentarily and deal informationally with the text and then move on to the formational mode. There is a necessary interplay between these two approaches to the scripture. But as far as the role of scripture in spiritual formation is concerned, you ultimately need to arrive at a disciplined development of the formational mode of approaching the text. Only in the formational mode, where that shift of the inner posture of our being takes place, can we become listeners. Only in that mode can we become receptive and accessible to be addressed by the living Word of God.

It is going to be difficult for you to move from one mode

into the other, especially from the informational to the formational. The temptation is to dispense with either the informational or the formational. There are those who throw out the informational dynamic, the whole scope of critical methods of biblical study as "liberal" or "humanistic" and have nothing to do with it. They attempt to come to the text only at the formational level. There are also those who throw out the formational dynamic, dismiss it as "fundamentalism," "subjectivism," or "pietism," and attempt to come to the text only on the informational level. Both dynamics are necessary. God asks to be loved with all our minds *and* all our hearts. The informational aspect relates primarily (though not exclusively) to our minds. It must be balanced with the formational aspect which relates primarily (though not exclusively) to our hearts.

Adrian van Kaam succinctly states the gist of what we have been considering in this chapter:

> To find self formation by means of scripture reading I must be open in docility to what its text may eventually tell me about myself; I must abide with formative reading until it yields to me its treasure. Formative reading implies, moreover, my willingness to change my current self in light of the formative insight scripture may radiate to me. The word as formative has the power to transform me. It can give rise to a new self in Christ, permeating all dimensions of my life. The word as formative can lift me beyond the stirrings of my ego and vital life so that I may discover my graced life form in the Eternal Word.[9]

I hope that by now you realize that this formational mode of reading not only breaks open your old perceptual framework of reading, but also calls for a new perspective toward scripture itself, the topic of our next area of consideration.

6.

The Iconographic Nature of Scripture

THE PROBLEM OF MEANING

*W*HETHER you realize it or not, we have been thinking about the hermeneutical endeavor, that is, the process of bringing meaning out of a text, especially scripture.

Behind the whole hermeneutical endeavor lies a danger. It is a presumption that has developed directly out of the informational dynamic of our culture. It is the presumption that meaning is communicated primarily, if not wholly, at the cognitive level of human existence. This presumption says if only we could merge the cognitive horizons of the New Testament writers with the cognitive horizon of the modern interpreter, then meaning could be communicated. If we adopt this perception of the transfer of understanding at a cognitive level, at an informational level only, then the only parameters we have with which to evaluate our understanding are our own self-generated parameters. This is why the Bible tends to be interpreted in the light of modern philosophical presumptions. We simply read back into the text our own world view in order to maintain our cognitive, rational control of the text.

In reaction to this trend, conservative biblical scholars have tended to stress the affective level of understanding. They say, "If only we can have what we believe is the same experience the New Testament church had, then we can automatically understand what they are communicating." But this presumption results in the varieties of diverse religious experiences becoming the norms of biblical interpretation.

The Wesleyan tradition offers a dynamic that can bridge this gap between the cognitive and affective polarities. It is found in Wesley's lifelong purpose to conjoin knowledge and vital piety. Wesley clearly saw that the cognitive and the affective dimensions of human existence must be conjoined in mutual interdependence if Christians were not going to fall into the extremes of sterile intellectualism on the one side or mindless enthusiasm on the other.

How does this relate to reading the Bible? Biblical writers utilized cognitive images from within their perceptual horizon to express the reality of their experience with God, their encounter with the Word, and its intrusion into their lives. Their images are cognitive portraits of an affective involvement with the living Word. They are the "knowledge" of a "vital piety." Now the images—the words, the phrases—which the New Testament writers used, necessarily contained the conditioning of their perceptual horizon. They were the words and phrases used in the "morning newspaper" in Athens or Corinth or Ephesus or Rome in the first century. However, there was a new and radically different level of communication to the readers who had also entered into the same experience with God.

DEEPER DIMENSIONS OF MEANING

Aelred Squire succinctly describes this aspect of the communication of meaning. He writes, "It is the man who lives a certain kind of life who is in a position to understand the doctrine. There are some kinds of knowledge to which experience is the only key."[1]

Paul, I think, expresses this same realization. In First Corinthians 1–2, he engages in a rather extended discussion on the contrast between the communication of the Gospel and the communication of philosophical knowledge. Paul first deals with philosophical wisdom vis-à-vis the proclamation of the Gospel (1:18–2:5). Then he writes, "We, too, speak wisdom" (2:6); and begins to amplify the nature of the wisdom he speaks (2:7–12). It is not a wisdom that correlates to the wisdom of developed human rationality. It is a wisdom that has its roots in the experience of the indwelling presence of God through the Holy Spirit. Paul closes his description of this wisdom by saying, "That which we communicate [referring back to 2:6], we communicate not in taught words of human wisdom but in taught spiritualities of the Spirit, expounding spiritual things" (2:13). He then continues, "The unspiritual person does not receive the things of the Spirit of God, for they are foolishness to such a one who is not able to understand because such things are spiritually discerned. But the spiritual person discerns all things" (2:14).

I believe that although Paul's verbal images—the words he uses in his writing, his proclamation, and his teaching—are images necessarily conditioned by the perceptual horizon of the first century world, Paul is saying that he uses these terms as the only linguistic means available to communicate to his Christian readers the deeper dynamics of their common experience of life shaped by the Word.

THE NATURE OF SCRIPTURE

Here is another way to look at this dynamic of the scripture. Alan Jones writes, "The journey [inward to God] involves the exploration of images, mythologies, ideas, pictures, in the hope that one or two many become an icon, a window into reality."[2] I believe you can turn this idea around and illustrate a profound truth about the nature of scripture. What, on the one hand, are icons for those whose lives are intimately involved in the reality portrayed by the text are, on the other hand, but pictures, ideas, myths, and images for those who still stand outside that reality.

I believe this is where the conundrum of biblical inter-pretation lies. No matter how perfectly we reproduce the perceptual horizon of the New Testament world as the con-text for understanding the terms and images utilized by the New Testament writers; no matter how objectively and accurately we reproduce the dynamics of human existence in that era; no matter how adequate our cognitive grasp of the life experience of the Christian community; unless we also participate in the experiential reality of life shaped by the living Word, our ultimate understanding of the New Testament writings will be one of seeing images, myths, ideas, and pictures which we can only analyze or "demy-thologize" in the light of our own experience of human ex-istence.

In scripture, we encounter God coming to us, address-ing us, penetrating our garbled, distorted, debased word, seeking to speak us forth as God's word into the world. But the Word addresses us in scripture through human com-munication, human language. So there is a sense in which scripture is iconographic. That may be an uncomfortable idea for you because iconography is rather alien to our Western perception and comprehension. Yet a realization of the iconographic nature of scripture is essential for our deepest understanding of scripture; it is vital to the role of scripture in our spiritual formation.

The writers of scripture were participants in a radically new order of being which was shaped by the living Word of God. Of necessity, they were constrained to utilize the lan-guage of the old order of being, the language of their world, to convey to one another the breadth and length and heighth and depth of their experience with the Word. But in doing this, language becomes iconographic. It be-comes a verbal window into the reality of life shaped by the Word.

The Roman-Hellenistic culture was a very iconographic culture. The art, the architecture, the coinage, the sculp-ture of the Roman-Hellenistic world served to portray for the people of that world the spiritual realms which were thought to form the context for human existence. It was an iconographic society, and Christianity employed this dimension in its writings.

Let me illustrate this literary iconography for you by looking at the New Testament terms for the church, that community shaped by the Word. When you simply try to list the New Testament terms for the church it is mind-boggling. All attempts to give a rational, logical, cognitive organization to these catagories meet with failure. That is the informational approach; and we are up against something here that eludes our rational, objective control. The church is described as: city, body, bride, temple, stone, building, house, vineyard, kingdom, nation, family, flock, God's people, army, sons of light, salt, leaven, firstborn, priest, servant, and on and on. Paul Minear described it well:

> No list can exhaust the vivid imaginative power of the NT writers or do justice to the fluidity, vitality, and subtlety of their conceptions. None of the separate titles or pictures can be taken as comprehending the total range of thought. None of them can be reduced to objective, qualifying definitions. [The informational approach[1]] These words and pictures are channels of thought rather than receptacles of ideas with fixed meanings. This is due, not alone to the character of the thinking, but also to the qualitative, relational character of the reality being described.[3]

Then Minear focuses precisely upon the truly iconographic nature of the New Testament imagery: "Participation in the life of the church was considered necessary for comprehending the implications of the pictures."[4] In other words, for those who lived within the reality of the new order of being established by God through Jesus and actualized by the presence and work of the Holy Spirit, for the community shaped by the Word, the multiple, diverse images of the church became icons through which they perceived and experienced ever new and deeper dimensions of the infinite reality of life shaped by encounter with and response to the living and productive Word of God.

65

THE DYNAMIC OF SCRIPTURE AS ICON

Scripture is iconographic. One of the interesting features of some icons is that the farther you look into the picture, the larger things become, rather than smaller. The next time you see an icon that has scenery, look closely. Look at the windows, for instance. There may be one window at the forefront of the icon which is relatively small. Then there may be another window, obviously in the background, which is much larger than the one in the foreground. Or look at the buildings. The buildings in the back tend to get bigger rather than smaller as we would expect. Do you see what this does? It totally reverses our normal artistic perspective in which the picture recedes to a vanishing point. We tend to judge icons by our ingrained sense of perspective. But icons turn our perspective around. When you look at an icon, you discover that the point of focus is in you, not "out there" in the picture. You find yourself drawn into a reality, a mystery, which opens out in front of you. Instead of being an independent, objective observer who retains control of the picture, you find that the icon conveys an independent, objective reality that encounters you, addresses you, and draws you into its order of being. This is why, for our Eastern and Russian Orthodox brothers and sisters, icons are so vital within the community of believers as windows into reality, drawing them into God's new order of being in Christ.

Iconography, therefore, is the perceptual framework I would like to suggest to you as your basic perception of scripture. Begin to think of scripture iconographically. You see, there is a sense in which the overload of the informational approach conditions the way we perceive what we read. The informational approach has basically geared us to dimensions like realistic art, where there is a point of diminishing returns "out there." There is a "zero point" from which everything comes to us, and we are in control. However, if we begin to see the scripture iconographically, automatically we begin to move into the formational mode. We stand before scripture, and it opens up before us; it addresses us. It draws us into that order of being that is shaped by the Word.

If iconography *is* a major dynamic of scripture, as Paul seems to be saying, then the informational approach must move to the formational approach if the Bible is to be a vehicle of spiritual formation, if it is to be an agent of encounter with and shaping by the Word of God. We must open ourselves before scripture receptively. We must listen. We must be ready to respond. When we approach the scriptures in this manner, we find ourselves drawn into that Life where our "word" begins to resonate with the Word. We begin to discover that all of the old structures of meaning, value, purpose, identity, fulfillment, and wholeness become turned around and begin to take radically new shapes. Our life begins to take on new meaning, new values, new purpose, new identity, because we are becoming the "word" God is speaking us forth to be in the world. We begin to live in the world, in our relationships with others, the life of the new order of being in Christ. We begin to become participants in kairotic existence.

Kairotic Existence

L ET us take a few moments, as we begin this chapter, to re-collect ourselves in the presence of God
and open our hearts, our lives, our minds, and our
beings to whatever it is God wants to do with us. Let us be
still in God's presence.

> O God, once again we turn to you. We come to you in our
> incompleteness that you might complete us. We come to you
> in our brokenness that you might make us whole. We come to
> you in our "dis-ease" that you might heal us. Help us to
> open the deeps of our lives to you, that in this chapter and in
> all of this book you may be able to work in us that which you
> purpose for us in your perfect will for our wholeness. Stir our
> hearts, stimulate our minds, have your way with us. For all
> you are doing, for all you are going to do, we give you praise
> and thanks, in Jesus' name. Amen.

We come now to another area of perceptual shift, another opening to an alternate perceptual awareness. If the
scripture can function iconographically in our lives, if it
can become a window through which we find ourselves
drawn into God's new order of being in Christ, then this

insight may call for the deepest perceptual shift of all. What is suggested is a perceptual shift that brings us to an awareness that the word God speaks us forth to be has a frame of reference in an order of being which, in many, many ways, is radically antithetical to that order of being which garbles, distorts, and debases our word.

THE "WORLD" OF THE SCRIPTURE

Let us begin by looking at a collage of Merton's insights into the relationship between the scripture and this alternate world of being.

> The Bible is without question one of the most unsatisfying books ever written—at least until the reader has come to terms with it in a very special way. But it is a difficult book to come to terms with. . . .
>
> Even to appreciate much of the Bible as literature one has to come to terms with the fact that it gives literary expression to an experience that is more than aesthetic. Not only is it beyond literature, it is also in a certain sense beyond "religion"—beyond the devout and cleansing awe of initiation into ritual and mystery, beyond the healing and transforming sense of moral self-transcendence.[1]

Do you begin to get the feel for the direction in which Merton is moving here? He is beginning to intimate that in the scripture you are encountering something that takes you beyond yourself. In part, Merton is illustrating the iconographic nature of scripture, but he is also pointing to a different mode of being.

> For most people, the understanding of the Bible is, and should be, a struggle: not merely to find meanings that can be looked up in books of reference *[the informational mode!]*, but to come to terms personally with the stark scandal and contradiction in the Bible itself *[the formational mode!]*. It should not be our aim merely to explain these contradictions away *[informational]*, but rather to use them as ways to *enter into the strange and paradoxical world of mean-*

70

ings and experiences that are beyond us and yet often extremely
and mysteriously relevant to us.[2]

It becomes clearer here that there is more than just an
idea presented in scripture. There is an alternate order of
being which confronts us. It draws us out of where we are
into something else.

> Thus we should realize that the Biblical message is some-
> thing that establishes and confirms a community, a convo-
> cation, in its identity. The common reaction of belief,
> response, acceptance, affirmation, praise and thanksgiv-
> ing by which the "word" is not simply understood but *cel-
> ebrated*, is essential to a full understanding of the Bible.[3]

Now we see what Merton is beginning to say. Up to this
point, I have been tracing his intimation that the Bible is
dealing with another order of being. Now he is saying that
the Bible shapes a community in that order of being and
that it is within that shaped community that we come to
full understanding of the scripture.

> At the very heart of the Bible is the theme of "passover"
> and exodus, the procession of the redeemed out of a
> doomed society into the desert, on the way to a promised
> kingdom. . . . And of course the true meaning of Easter is
> precisely that the Christian is called to make this journey
> with Christ and the people of God out of "Egypt" to the
> promised land.[4]

Then, using the black church in Faulkner's *The Sound and
the Fury* as an illustration, Merton writes:

> Set precariously on the very edge of the world, [it] is an
> eschatological symbol of the redeemed community. And
> those who "hear" the secret invitation gather together
> there spontaneously to form an *ekklesia*, to understand and
> celebrate the word of liberation.[5]

Dilsey listens to a black preacher leave his intellectual style
and come alive to the gospel.

The corresponding transformation in Dilsey is completely Biblical. It is the fruit of an inner ripening which we have sensed in her all along. This is her *kairos,* her time of illumination and unburdening, her meeting with the creative and redemptive power of the Spirit which shows her all the world.[6]

Merton speaks here not only of the community of the new order of being in Christ, but also of the individual whose life is hid in that new order of being.

Squire also speaks of this deeper reality:

He [Hugh of St. Victor] sees himself and those he is teaching as *living in the world of Scripture,* since there is, after all, no other world to live in as far as the Christian is concerned, living, as he does, "in the age to which all the ages have been leading up." It is in this and like phrases, that St. Paul expresses the Christian conviction that the last age of Scripture is already working itself out in faith. Thus the Scriptures open upon the ultimate and the God of Scripture is not time-bound.[7]

What Squire and Merton are sharing with us is something that Paul exhorts us to in both Ephesians and Colossians. The Letter to the Ephesians divides itself very neatly into two halves. The first half is doctrinal; the second half is practical. In the first half, Paul is setting forth the great mystery of God in Christ and what it means for us. Then, beginning in chapter four, Paul starts speaking about "walking." He begins in 4:1, "I urge you, therefore, as a prisoner of the Lord, to *walk* worthy of the calling with which you were called." He elaborates on that for sixteen verses and then, in 4:17, says, "This I say and witness in the Lord: you must no longer *walk* as the Gentiles in the emptiness of their minds." In 5:2, Paul exhorts, "*Walk* in love." And finally, in 5:15, "Look carefully, therefore, how you *walk.*" What Paul is communicating in his repeated use of the word *walk* is the whole ordering of one's life, the whole ordering of your being in the world.

Notice the nature of the walk in Ephesians 5:15: "Look

carefully, therefore, how you walk, not as unwise but as wise." In our informational culture, we tend to think of wisdom as a cognitive function. We use as synonyms for wisdom such terms as: intelligent, brilliant, genius. These may be adjuncts of wisdom, but biblically, and especially for Paul and his Hebrew tradition, wisdom is the ordering of your life according to the will and purpose of God. Wisdom is bringing all the dynamics of your being into harmony with the word God is speaking you forth to be in the world.

Paul then adds one qualifying phrase to further clarify the nature of walking in wisdom, an extremely significant phrase. Translations of verse 16 usually say something like, "making the most of the time." The greek is *exagoradzomenoi ton kairon*, a phrase which appears again in Colossians 4:5, in exactly the same form and again in the context of walking in wisdom. Hidden in the middle of the long word, *exagoradzomenoi* is the word *agora*: the marketplace. The verb *agoradzo* expresses the activity one carried out in the *agora*. It meant "to buy," "to sell," "to conduct business." In this context, *exagoradzo* had a very particular meaning. It literally means "to buy out." If you went into a family's stall or shop and bought everything they had, you would *exagoradzo* them; you would buy them out.

Now Greek is such a highly inflected language you can say very precise things with it when you want to. Paul seems to be doing that here. He is using what is known as the "middle voice" of the verb which means that the subject is acting on or for itself. In this case the most logical translation of *exagoradzomenoi* would be, "to fully buy up for yourself," or "to fully appropriate for yourself."

But "fully appropriate *what* for yourself?" Paul says, "the *kairos*." In Greek there are two words for time. One is the word *chronos*, from which we get "chronometer," "chronology," and all those clock-type words. *Chronos* is basically the sequential flow of seconds, minutes, hours, days, years.

Kairos, however, although it is sometimes used as a synonym for *chronos*, is a term that usually means "the fulfilled time," "the crucial time," "the decisive time," that time when everything flows together and an opportunity is there which, perhaps, can never be seized again.

In the New Testament use of this term, and particularly in Paul's writings, there is a very interesting sequence of usage. *Kairos* is used very focally in two ways. First, it is used with respect to what God has done in Christ.[8] In some sense, the life, death, resurrection, and ascension of Jesus is the *kairos* of God. For example, Mark, as he conveys to us the encapsulated version of Jesus' message, reports Jesus as saying, "The *kairos* is fulfilled. The Kingdom of God has come" (1:15). Mark is reporting what the rest of the New Testament affirms: in Christ, God's decisive moment in human history has come to fulfillment. In Christ, God's new order of being—the kingdom of God—has broken into human history.

Second, another New Testament dimension of *kairos* refers to the return of Christ.[9] There will be that culminating *kairos*, that consummating *kairos*, in which God will bring to fruition the work that was begun in the initial *kairos*, in the incarnation, death, resurrection, and ascension of Jesus.

Along with these two usages, we find Paul, in many places (Eph. 5:16 and Col. 4:5 are among the clearest of all), using *kairos* as though it has something to do with the very context of Christian existence in the world.[10] In some sense, Paul seems to be indicating that Christians, as they live their lives in the world, are living in an order of being that was inaugurated in the incarnation of Jesus and will be consummated in his return.

When Paul says, "Fully appropriate for yourselves the *kairos*" (Eph. 5:16, Col. 4:5), he is saying that we are to fully appropriate for ourselves, to completely immerse ourselves, to totally consecrate ourselves, to unconditionally yield ourselves to this new order of being in Christ which God offers. We are to allow our daily life to be shaped by the dynamics of that new order of being—by its values and structures, by its pervading reality of the presence, purpose, and power of God.

Live *kairotically,* Paul is saying. Again the Greek is beautiful because the use of the tenses can be very significant. The tense Paul uses here is the one for continuing action. Paul doesn't say, "Go out and do this as a one-time event;" Paul is saying, "*Continually* appropriate for yourselves the *kairos*." Christian existence is kairotic existence.

The *kairos* of God's transforming grace, the *kairos* of the new order of being which God has provided in Christ, the *kairos* of an order of being shaped by the living Word of God is the "world" of the scripture. Kairotic existence is life lived in that world: life in which the word God speaks us forth to be is shaped by God's living Word.

SOME DYNAMICS OF KAIROTIC EXISTENCE

In the rest of the passage in Ephesians 5, Paul goes on to give us some of the dynamics of kairotic existence. He tells us first, "Do not be ignorant, but understand the will of the Lord" (5:17). The primary element in kairotic existence is the will of the Lord. Kairotic existence is a life in the world which is shaped by the will of God.

Secondly, Paul says, "Do not be drunk with wine, which is 'unsalvation,'[11] but be filled with the Spirit" (5:18). Kairotic existence is not only life shaped by the will of God, it is also a life empowered by the indwelling presence of God.

The third aspect of this kairotic existence becomes very crucial for us in our individualistic, individualizing, and privatizing culture. When Paul says, "Speaking to one another in psalms and hymns and spiritual songs" (5:19), he is portraying kairotic existence as life in community. When Paul writes of speaking to one another in songs, hymns, and spiritual songs, somehow I have difficulty picturing the Christian community as the local opera guild. I believe Paul meant that kairotic existence is a way of life in the world in which our lives become harmonious for others. It doesn't mean we all "sing the same tune." It doesn't mean we all have to "sing the melody." We each have our own part to "sing" in relationship with others, but our part will be a nurturing harmony in the lives of others. When we are seeking to become the word God speaks us forth to be in the lives of others, that word will ultimately be a harmonious word because it is a word for their wholeness.

Fourth, Paul concludes his description of kairotic existence as, "Singing and 'psalming' in your hearts to the Lord, giving thanks in everything in the name of our Lord Jesus Christ to God the Father, being submissive to one another" (5:19–21). Kairotic existence is the state of being harmoniously in relationship with God. It is thankfully open and receptive to the shaping purpose of God in all the circumstances of life. It is humbly yielded to being the word God speaks forth for others.

In Colossians 4:5, where Paul also exhorts us to "fully appropriate for ourselves the *kairos*," there is one element that Paul adds to the phrase which helps to define and clairfy more sharply what he is saying about kairotic existence. He says, "Walk in wisdom," the same general dynamic of life seen in Ephesians 5:15, where he says, "Look carefully, therefore, how you walk, not as unwise but as wise." In Colossians, however, Paul adds, "Walk in wisdom *toward those outside,* fully appropriating for yourselves the *kairos.*" There are two orders of being here. There are those who, by the yielding of themselves to God's encounter and intrusion into their lives, have been drawn into kairotic existence and are in the process of being drawn ever more deeply into the wholeness and fulness of that kairotic existence. And there are those who have not responded positively to God and stand outside.

Notice that when Paul says, "Walk in wisdom toward those outside," this is not some sort of judgmental, "ivory-towerish" isolationism, or separatism. Paul is saying in a very profound way that for those who have set their feet upon the journey into wholeness in Christ, an essential part of that journey is becoming the agent of God's wholeness into the broken life of the world. As our lives interact with the world, we are to *be* the *kairos* of God in the life of the world. Or, in John's words, "As he [Christ] is, so are we in this world" (1 John 4:17, RSV).

THE RHYTHMS OF KAIROTIC EXISTENCE

We have considered some of the characteristics of kairotic existence: the will of the Lord, filled with the Spirit, harmony, thankfulness, humility, and submissiveness. But there are also certain rhythms of kairotic existence that are of focal concern to those of us who are hungering for deeper spiritual life.

One basic rhythm of kairotic existence is the rhythm of spiritual discipline. Perhaps there is some point where God is speaking to you, showing you it is necessary for you to die to self and not seek to maintain your own rhythms of life in the face of an Ultimate Rhythm. Perhaps the Living Word is calling you to exercise a spiritual discipline of submissiveness to God and humility in response to a Deeper Rhythm that is not as compatible with your normal rhythm of spiritual life as you would like. Spiritual disciplines take place at those points in our lives where the dynamics of kairotic existence confront our "word" in its garbled, distorted, and debased condition, where the living, penetrating Word of God probes the depths of our being.

Ultimately, spiritual disciplines are not something we choose for ourselves. This is another problem we have in our individualized, privatized form of religion in our culture. We think spiritual disciplines are something *we take on*. We decide we need to grow in some particular area of our spiritual life, so we set to work in this area and develop some "spiritual disciplines." The only problem is that when we develop our own spiritual disciplines, they have a way of being compatible with who we are and what we are. I don't mind taking up the cross and following the Lord as long as I can choose when I'm going to take it up and who will see it and praise me for it. Even though such disciplines may not be easy, I can handle them as long as I'm getting those kinds of ego boosts by being allowed to do it my own way.

Genuine spiritual disciplines are disciplines that intrude into our lives at points where we are in bondage to some-

thing that garbles, debases, and distorts the word God
speaks us forth to be. These disciplines occur in our bondage to our own brokenness from which God is seeking to
liberate us. At this level, spiritual disciplines are not comfortable. Spiritual disciplines are a grace of God. Spiritual
disciplines come to us from God. We may not initially see
them as coming from God's hand; but once we have sub-
mitted ourselves humbly to them, have become responsive
to the disciplines, and have begun to experience the
growth and wholeness they bring, we begin to realize they
are a gift of God. They are God's doing all along—not our
own.

Another rhythm of kairotic existence, therefore, is the
rhythm of community, the rhythm of life together in
Christ. Since spiritual disciplines are not always pleasant,
we need the community of faith. This is the deeper dimension of bearing one another's burdens and building one
another up. I know that, in myself, I do not have the
strength to maintain the necessary spiritual disciplines I
need for growth into wholeness in Christ. I know that
when the going gets tough, my desire for *my* will, *my* desires, *my* purposes, and *my* comfort, are going to subvert
and pervert those spiritual disciplines unless I have brothers and sisters in Christ who hold me to the task. Unless I
have either a spiritual director or a spiritual formation
group to whom I am accountable, I will not persevere in
the disciplines. I will fall short. You see, the kairotic community is not some private little club that we so often tend
to make the Christian community. It is a community
shaped by the living Word of God in which persons are
nurtured into the wholeness God is speaking them forth to
be in the world.

Yet another rhythm of kairotic existence is liturgy. We
protestants certainly have lost an essential dimension of
kairotic existence in our historic resistance to liturgy. Fortu-
nately, there is a movement back to more holistic liturgy.
Liturgy is a prescribed rite for public worship. Yet it is
more. It becomes the corporate lifestyle of the kairotic community through which it seeks to allow God to bring it into
the full expression of its kairotic existence in relationship

with God, with one another, and with the world. Liturgy is a means of grace in which God more fully speaks forth into being the human community, binds them more closely to himself in love, bonds them more closely to one another in love, and thrusts them into the world as agents of God's love. Liturgy is the life-breath of kairotic existence, the heartbeat of the kairotic community.

All of these rhythms—spiritual disciplines, community, liturgy—are rhythms that thrust us out into the world. They are rhythms by which we bring the world that is in us into the presence of God so it may be transformed. Then, in that experience of God's transforming grace, we bring the kairotic existence of grace and love into the world as agents of healing, of wholeness, of reconciliation, and of love.

Spiritual formation, therefore, is the process of learning to live kairotically. It is the process of beginning to live, increasingly, day by day, this kairotic existence—an existence of having the word God speaks us forth to be shaped and fulfilled by the living Word of God. I hope that you now see that the scripture is one of the major vehicles of the intrusion, the address, the transforming encounter with the *kairos*, with the realm of the Word, with God. The scripture is one of the major vehicles for the action of the presence, the power, the purpose of God in our lives and in our communities of faith. Scripture is an icon through which the reality of kairotic existence penetrates to the core of our being and calls us forth from our garbled, distorted, debased word to the word God speaks us forth to be in the world.

We have now completed our consideration of four focal aspects of our perceptual framework that affect the role of scripture in spiritual formation.

1. We have sought to develop an alternate perception of self-image by viewing ourselves as "words" God speaks forth into the world, "words" that must be shaped by the living Word of God if our garbled, debased, distorted "word" is to become the liberating, healing, redemptive, loving "word" God speaks us forth to be in the lives of others.

2. We have seen that if the scripture is to become the living, productive Word of God that penetrates to the core of our garbled, distorted, debased "word," we need to develop a formational perspective toward reading the scripture (in balance with our informational approach) so that we become open, receptive, and responsive to encounter with the Word of God in scripture.

3. We have also seen that approaching the scripture formationally is enhanced by a perception of the iconographic nature of scripture, perceiving scripture as a window into the reality of a radically new order of being in Christ.

4. Finally, we have seen that the iconographic nature of scripture leads us to a new perception of Christian existence as kairotic existence in which the shaping of our "word" by the Word of God takes place.

III.

FOCAL EXPERIENTIAL SHIFTS

8.

Functional-Relational Dynamics

FOR the last four chapters we have been wrestling with some vital perceptual dynamics that directly shape (or misshape) our spiritual formation. More significantly, these perceptual dynamics condition the role of scripture in our spiritual formation. We have examined alternative perceptual frameworks for viewing ourselves and the Word of God, our dynamics of reading, our perspective of scripture, and the deeper dynamics of Christian life. Having examined these aspects of our *perceptual* framework, we now must consider some *experiential* dynamics that deeply determine the shape of our lives and, consequently, powerfully shape (or misshape) our spiritual formation.

There are two basic forms of experiential dynamics: cultural and religious, which, of course, interplay with each other. Rather than artificially separating the cultural and religious aspects, I will attempt to combine both as I share with you some thoughts on two focal polarities of our experiential dynamics.

THE FUNCTIONAL DYNAMICS OF OUR CULTURE

The first polarity is Functional-Relational. Western culture in general, and American culture in particular, is a functionally oriented culture. Listen to a conversation between two strangers. Before many minutes pass, sometimes seconds, one will usually ask the other, "What do you do?" This is the question that establishes identity, the question that enables us to rank a person in our system of values. Our culture establishes the meaning, the value, the purpose, even the self-image of persons on the basis of function.

The destructive nature of this functional orientation manifests itself in various ways in our culture. One area is seen in teenage suicide, the group with the highest suicide rate in the culture. It is well known that a major factor in suicide is a profound sense of meaninglessness and purposelessness, a loss or personal value and self-image. The youth of our culture are being raised in a culture which, as just noted, values persons on the basis of their function. They are also being raised in a culture that tends to postpone meaningful functional activity until the early or midtwenties (the cut-off line for the highest suicide rate!). Thus our youth are caught in a tremendous "Catch-22" situation: their value, meaning, identity, and purpose depend on their functional role in society, but they are not allowed to have a significant functional role. Is it any wonder that suicide, drug abuse, and crime all have their peak representation in this age group?

Another manifestation of the destructive consequences of the functional orientation is seen at the other end of the social spectrum—the retired. For some time, I have suspected that if the facts were known they would reveal that another peak in the suicide statistics appears in the retired bracket. The problem is that the retired are more skilled in masking their suicide so as to avoid various problems for their families. Recently, while sharing this hypothesis in a conference, a geriatric social worker who had been studying research in this area broke into my presentation and

confirmed my hypothesis. Consider the situation of the retired. One morning they wake up and the functional role
which, for a lifetime, has given their life meaning, value,
purpose, and identity is no longer there. The functional
support structure for their sense of self-image and self-
esteem is gone. It is no wonder that depression is almost
epidemic among the retired and that suicide is prevalent.

One final manifestation of the destructive consequences
of the functional orientation is found in the suddenly
handicapped or unemployed. They, too, find themselves
without the functional role, which has given their lives
meaning, value, and purpose.

THE FUNCTIONAL DYNAMIC IN THE CHURCH

In the Christian community I have encountered some
heart-rending examples of the damaging power of the
functional dynamic. At the seminary where I teach, we
have a program of supervised ministries in which most of
the students have to engage in three semesters of practical
ministry in various settings: hospitals, prisons, nursing
homes, social agencies, as well as churches. The students
spend eight hours a week in ministry and then engage in a
reflection seminar every week. During each semester, students present two case studies on two of their experiences
of ministry.

One semester a most interesting pattern developed in
the reflection seminar for which I was the moderator. The
case studies for each week described situations in which
the students had been called upon to be an agent of Christ
in their setting. In each instance, the students had worked
out a "plan of attack" in preparation for the ministry. They
had their functional agenda very carefully worked out. In
each instance, however, when the students arrived at the
place of ministry, there was something in the situation that
completely thwarted their carefully developed functional
agenda. The first thing the students would try to do was to
adjust the functional agenda. Sometimes they would try
two or three different functional modes in an attempt to
minister, and each would fail. In each instance, the stu-

dents were devastated. Some were brought to the point of seriously questioning whether or not they belonged in the ministry. For them, functional failure was equated with failure in ministry. Ministry, together with their self-identity, value, meaning, purpose as a minister, was inseparably related to the effectiveness of their functional activities.

In one case, the head nurse asked a student if he would please go down and talk with a relative of hers who was terminally ill. This particular student was locked into a verbal functioning mode of ministry. He had planned to give the patient some scriptures of comfort, lead him into a discussion of the state of his soul and his readiness for death, and have prayer with him. When the student entered the room he found the person lying in bed, conscious but practically comatose, unable to respond. The student started talking to the body on the bed. The body just lay there and stared unblinkingly at the ceiling. The student asked if he would like to have prayer. No response. The student started a tentative prayer, opened one eye to see if there was any response: no response. The student stopped praying and, after trying several other approaches to ministry, got up and walked out.

He was practically destroyed, and came to the seminar seriously questioning whether or not he should be in ministry since he couldn't function. As he began to work through this situation, with the help of the reflection seminar, he began to see that ministry is more than what one does. He began to see that ministry is what one *is* in relationship with God in service to others. He had begun to see how damaging the *functional* determination of self-identity, meaning, value, and purpose can be.

Dr. Edward E. Thornton, professor of Psychology of Religion at Southern Baptist Theological Seminary, made a most interesting remark in a lecture a couple of years ago.[1] He said that until recently the dynamics of pastoral care in seminaries and in the field have been basically functional in their orientation. That is, what do you *do* to help a person in crisis? What do you *do* to meet the needs of a person? Then he noted that in recent years there has been a shift to the realization that what one does may not be as important as who one is with that person. He was indicating that leaders in the field of pastoral counseling are beginning to realize that there needs to be a shift from a functional mode to a relational mode.

FUNCTIONAL DYNAMICS IN SPIRITUAL FORMATION

Let's make this very pertinent; here is where the shoe may begin to pinch a little bit. For those of us seriously engaged in spiritual formation, there is a strong temptation to see spiritual formation as a technique that we do. We may even be seeing spiritual formation as something we *do* to revive a burned-out ministry. We may be seeing spiritual formation as something we *do* to replace worn-out methods of devotion or worship. How often do we see worship as something we *do* to get right with God, instead of an offering of ourselves in worship through which God can draw us into the depths of his loving presence. This functional dynamic threads its way throughout our lives, including our "spiritual" activities.

Here is the point at issue for us: the danger of using scripture in spiritual formation as an instrument or technique. What do I *do* with scripture to get spiritually formed? This is why we still have not yet come to the specific role of scripture in spiritual formation. Before we can consider the role of scripture in spiritual formation we must work through the shifts of perceptual framework we have already considered and shifts of experiential dynamics we are now considering.

Let me give you a scriptural example of the danger of the functional approach and the biblical alternative. The example comes from Matthew 3:16–4:4, the beginning of Jesus' ministry:

> Having been baptized, Jesus immediately went up from the water, and behold, the heavens were opened and he saw the Spirit descending upon him as a dove. And behold, a voice from heaven said, "This is my beloved son, with whom I am well pleased." Then Jesus was led into the

desert by the Spirit to be tested by the Devil. And he fasted forty days and forty nights, and afterward he was hungry. And the Tester came and said to him, "If you are the Son of God, speak in order that these stones might become bread." But he, answering, said, "It is written, 'Humanity shall not live by bread alone, but by every word which proceeds from the mouth of God.'"

Now there are two elements involved in Jesus' baptism. One is the element of empowerment. Jesus receives empowerment for ministry through the anointing of the Holy Spirit. It is beyond our range of focus to investigate the theological dimensions of Jesus' relationship to the Holy Spirit in his human existence prior to this event. However, there is at least, at this point, an overt awareness of his empowerment by the Spirit of God.

The second element is Jesus' call. Jesus receives his call through the heavenly voice which says, "You are my Son." Here again the theological question of Jesus' relationship to God in his human existence before this moment is beyond our focus. But here, too, there is, in this event, Jesus' clear awareness of his call to be God's son in his earthly life. Jesus' baptism is an experience of both empowerment for and call to ministry.

Jesus' temptation flows directly out of his empowerment and call. The event gives us a new insight into temptation. We tend to think of temptation as something that comes from outside. Temptation is seen as something foreign and external to life in Christ. But this is not the case. Temptations come right at the very heart of our life in Christ; they deal with its very nature. Jesus' temptation comes from his empowerment and his call. The result of his empowerment is that the very Spirit who empowers him *leads him out to be tested*. Wrestle with that one for a while! The nature of the testing focuses upon the call. Notice that Satan said to Jesus, "*If* you are *the Son of God* . . ." That is the call—"You are my Son." So we see that the temptation brings together both the empowerment and the call.

The temptation is for Jesus to use his empowerment to authenticate for himself his call; to use the power of the

Spirit to do something to prove for himself that he is the son of God. The temptation is for Jesus to find his role-affirmation, his self-identity, his value, meaning, and purpose through a functional approach. He is tempted to *do* something to prove who he is. This is our primary temptation in a functionally oriented society in a high-tech culture.

Consider Jesus' answer: "Human beings do not live by bread alone." Obviously bread is necessary, but "not by bread *alone*." Jesus is pointing to a deeper context of existence: human beings live "by every word which comes forth from God." Jesus' response to the *functional* temptation is to point to the *relational* reality of life. At the center, human life is set within a relationship with God. God's purpose becomes focal. God's action becomes central. The functional dynamic becomes a response to the Word God speaks into the situation at hand.

When Jesus says that we "shall not live by bread alone but by every word which proceeds from God," he is quoting from Deuteronomy 8:3. Have you ever looked carefully at this chapter? It is very interesting because it points up the dichotomy between the functional and relational dynamics of human life.

Deuteronomy 8 starts off looking very functional. *"All the commandments which I am commanding you today you shall be careful to do,* that you may live and multiply and go in and possess the land which the Lord your God swore to give to your fathers"(8:1). This seems to be totally functional: do this so that certain results may follow. But immediately the focus becomes relational: "You shall remember all the way the Lord your God has led you these forty years in the wilderness, that he might humble you, testing you to know what was in your heart. . . . He humbled you and let you hunger and fed you with manna" (8:2–3).

The account goes on to tell what *God* did, not what *they* did. God is leading them into a relational mode of life.

God is bringing you into a good land, a land of brooks of water, of fountains and springs, flowing forth in valleys and hills, a land of wheat and barley, . . . a land in which

> you will eat bread without scarcity, in which you will lack
> nothing. . . . And when you have eaten and are satisified,
> you shall bless the Lord your God for the good land he has
> given you.
>
> —Deuteronomy 8:7–10

Their life and welfare are the result of God's action, not theirs; the result of their relationship with God, not their functional activity.

Then look at the shift in the middle of the chapter: "Beware lest you forget the Lord your God," a warning against losing the relational focus of their lives; "By not keeping his commandments and his ordinances and his statutes" (8:11), the loss of the functional activity which rightly flows from the relationship focus. Then we see the final shift to the functional focus.

> Lest, when you have eaten and are full, and have built
> goodly houses and live in them, and when your herds and
> flocks multiply, and your silver and gold is multiplied, and
> all that you have is multiplied . . . you say in your heart,
> "My power and the might of my hand have gotten me this
> wealth."
>
> —Deuteronomy 8:12–13, 17, RSV

The contrast is between the sustenance of life which results from obedience to God, relational; and the results of functional self-effort, trying to bring about sustenance of life or presuming that such sustenance is the result of one's own self-effort.

It is out of this passage, where this contrast is set forth, that Jesus selects his response to the temptation: we do not live by functional dynamics alone but by our relationship with God.

THE FUNCTIONAL-RELATIONAL DYNAMICS OF SCRIPTURE

When Jesus says we live "by every Word which comes forth from God," he provides the focus for what we are seeking to do in this book. True life and wholeness are the results of being shaped by the Word of God. This shaping however, is not something we do by our own efforts (functional); it is what God does in us when we are in a loving, receptive, responsive *relationship* with God. The scripture is not something we can use to bring our lives into conformity with the image of God (functional), but something God can use to transform our garbled, distorted, debased "word" into the word God speaks us forth to be in the world (relational). If the scripture is to become such an instrument of God in our lives, however, we must shift from a functional to a relational mode of approach to the scripture.

Now we must recognize, just as when we considered information versus formation, that the functional and relational dynamics are not antithetical, or that one is bad and the other is good. It is a matter of the priority of the relational over the functional and the interrelationship between the two in a culture which has its priorities reversed. Our culture tends to think that our relational dynamics flow from our functional activities. But the biblical, the kairotic perspective, is that our functional activities must flow from our relational dynamics, especially our relationship with God.

One of the places where this reality is so awesomely revealed is at the end of the Sermon on the Mount, Matthew 7:21–23. Jesus says, "Not every one who says to me, 'Lord, Lord,' shall enter into the Kingdom of Heaven" (RSV). Surprisingly, Jesus seems to be saying that you can't rely simply on the relational dynamic for your salvation. "Not every one who says to me, 'Lord, Lord,' shall enter . . . but he who does the will of my Father who is in heaven" (RSV). Jesus seems to be making it all functional, all based on our *doing* the will of God. But then he goes on, "On that day many will say to me, 'Lord, Lord,'" claiming that relationship, "Did we not prophesy in your name, and cast out demons in your name, and do many mighty works in your name?" (RSV). Talk about having the functional dynamics all together! These people had developed the functional dynamics to the optimum. They would certainly have been called "super-Christians" by observers. But look at Jesus'

91

response: "I never knew you; depart from me, you evil-doers" (RSV).

"*I never knew you!*" Jesus makes the relational dynamic the foundation of the functional. In doing this, Jesus makes a crucial distinction between "evil-doing" and "doing evil." "Doing evil" is doing that which is contrary to the purpose of God. "Evil-doing," however, is doing that which is in harmony with the purpose of God (such as mighty works in Jesus' name, prophesying, exorcism) but doing it without a relationship with God; to do God's purpose in our own strength, in our own wisdom, in our own time, according to our own purposes. This is the essence of the functional mode when it becomes primary. The people Jesus was describing were doing great things, great "religious" things. Functionally they had it all together. But what they were doing did not flow out of their relationship with God. They were seeking to live by bread alone rather than by every Word which comes forth from God.

IMPACT ON OUR SPIRITUAL FORMATION

Our disciplines must emerge from our relationship with God if they are to be truly forming and not misforming, truly shaping and not misshaping. The first thing that happens if our spiritual disciplines don't emerge from our relationship with God is that they become a form, a very subtle and destructive form, of works-righteousness. They become a means by which we either attempt to transform ourselves into the image of God or attempt to gain God's favor. This means that our use of scripture in spiritual formation must also be unselfishly rooted in our relationship with God.

Merton says, "When the living relationship with God hardens into a rigid and 'established system' that claims to give man full control of all the answers and encourages him to 'use' even God for his own purposes, [an excellent description of the functional dynamic] then nature and culture, law and religion and even prophesy become ambiguous, deceptive, fatal not only to man but to man's ability to apprehend the truth of God."[2] He seems to be saying that the functional dynamic becomes a destructive hindrance to genuine relationship with God. Merton then goes on to show the relational dependence on the *kairos,* "the special, critical time, is then not only a time of breakthrough, convergence, the destruction of the old, the invasion by the new and unforeseen—it is above all *a time of decisive response*."[3] That is, it is relational!

It seems, therefore, that the first and continuing question of spiritual formation is: Are we operating on a functional basis, somehow trying to get ourselves closer to God or to what we think God wants us to be; or are we operating on a relational basis, where, in responsiveness to God, we are allowing God to draw us into genuine spiritual formation? Are we seeking to use the scripture as a means by which we can draw closer to God, a schedule of functional activities that will enable us to be what God wants us to be? Or are we seeking to come to the scripture openly, receptively, responsively; yielding ourselves to whatever God may want to say, and then obeying in such a way that our functional activities flow from our relationship with God? Do we come to the scripture seeking a technique, a methodology that will enable us to draw closer to God—a functional mode; or do we come to the scripture to open, to yield, to submit, to humble ourselves, to bow ourselves in God's presence, and allow God to speak to us and then to be obedient? Do we seek to function out of our relationship with God, or do we try to function ourselves into relationship with God?

Let me leave you with this. During your solitude today, during your quiet moments, I hope you will be able to take half an hour or so to be still and let God say whatever he wants to say to you about this. Here we are getting into something that goes down to the core of your being. Let the Lord analyze you. What is you primary mode of Christian life: is it functional or is it relational?

9.

Being and Doing

TAKE a few moments again to refocus your life, your attention, your centering before God. Open yourself to what God wants to do with you in this chapter.

Almighty God, we thank you for the ways in which you have been stretching us, the ways in which you have been breaking into what we thought were safe and secure areas of our being and opening us up to new depths and new areas of life and wholeness. We thank you that we have another opportunity now to open ourselves to your transforming touch. Help us, O God, to let you do whatever you want to do in our lives. Help us to say yes to you at the center of our being. In Jesus' name we pray. Amen.

We come now to the consideration of the second area of experiential dynamics in which we need a shift of focus if we are to experience holistic spiritual formation: the dynamics of being and doing. There is, of course, a close correlation between the dynamics of being-doing and those of functional-relational, which we looked at in the previous chapter. However, there is also a deeper dimension involved in being and doing—a dimension that probes the depths of who we are. Functional-relational dynamics can be considered without a probing disclosure of who we are. We are simply the person who relates or functions. Being-doing, however, requires that we come to grips with the inner parameters of who we are.

THE BIBLICAL PERSPECTIVE ON BEING AND DOING

Perhaps one of the sharpest New Testament foci on being and doing is in Matthew 23:25–28, where Jesus makes a powerful distinction between the outer appearance of "doing" and the inner reality of "being."

> Woe to you, scribes and Pharisees, hypocrites! for you cleanse the outside of the cup and of the plate, but inside they are full of extortion and rapacity. You blind Pharisee! first cleanse the inside of the cup and of the plate, that the outside also may be clean.
> Woe to you, scribes and Pharisees, hypocrites! for you are like whitewashed tombs, which outwardly appear beautiful, but within they are full of dead men's bones and all uncleanness. So you also outwardly appear righteous to men, but within you are full of hypocrisy and iniquity (RSV).

The Pharisees' problem, basically, was not simply a functional approach applied to their relationship with God, but the idea that "doing" somehow guaranteed the quality of "being" which God expected. They not only emphasized "doing" as the means of being in right relationship with God; they also emphasized "doing" as the means of "being" all God expected them to be. Look at Paul's litany of "doings" as a Pharisee in Philippians 3:4–6, which ends with the boast, "As to righteousness under the law blameless" (RSV). Unfortunately, we have not moved much further than the Pharisees in our religious communities. We, too, develop various lists of "do's" and "don'ts." We tell people, "Now that you have become a believer, a Christian, now that you have been born again," (or whatever phrases we use) "you have been regenerated—now you don't do 'those' things any more, you do 'these' instead." We give them our list of "do's" and "don'ts." We tell them, "If you are a good Christian, you do the do's and don't the don'ts. Otherwise, you are in trouble."

One of the problems with this, of course, is that serious and sensitive persons who genuinely attempt to "do the do's and don't the don'ts" immediately discover their inability to accomplish such a goal. This is what I see Paul wrestling with in Romans 7:15–25. As we have already noted in chapter 4, there is a wide diversity among biblical scholars on this passage. One group says this is Paul *before* he became a Christian. The rest of us believe this is Paul *after* he became a Christian. I believe most Christians will agree that Paul's description has been their experience since coming to life in Christ. We want to do the good, but, like Paul, we find ourselves doing the very thing we hate. We want to do what the word God speaks us forth to be ought to do, but find our garbled, distorted, debased word still speaking loudly. Wretched man that I am, wretched woman that I am, who will deliver me? This reality focuses our attention not upon doing but upon being. We sense that the failure is not at the "doing" level; as Paul said, there is another dynamic at work deep within us which militates against our "doing" what we want to do as disciples of Christ (see Rom. 7:23).

JESUS' FOCUS ON BEING AND DOING

Jesus' Great Commandment puts being and doing in their true relationship. Jesus was asked what the greatest commandment was, and he said, "You shall love the Lord your God with all your heart, and with all your soul, and with all your mind, and with all your strength" (Mark 12:30, RSV). Jesus is giving us several different insights here, all of which have to do with the relationship between being and doing. Once again, as with informational-formational and functional-relational, let me stress that I am not saying that "being" is everything and "doing" is nothing. I am saying that it is a matter of balance between being and doing; but the focus, the primary element, is being. This is what we see in the Great Commandment.

Jesus says, "Love God with all your heart, soul, mind, and strength." I want to work back in to Jesus' command from the outermost layer. What is loving God with all your strength? Your "strength," biblically, is your lifestyle. It is your actions. It is the outer manifestation in the world of who you are, in your relationships with others and in your interactions with the events and circumstances of your life. So to love God with all your strength is to seek to conform your life to God's standards or to what somebody tells you are God's standards—the list of "do's" and "don'ts." We try to love God with all our strength by doing what those who love God should do.

For example, perhaps in the development of our list of "do's," we discover that we are to love our enemies. It may take us a while to get that one onto our list, but there it is. Being good Christians and wanting to love God with all our strength, we put "love your enemy" up there on our "do" list. Of course, nobody has an enemy like ours! It is that cantankerous next-door neighbor, that obnoxious fellow employee, that intolerable boss, that exasperating church member. But we *have* to love them. So we begin to "love" them. We smile a lot when we are near them. We begin to be "happy" in their presence. We speak to them softly and listen patiently to their "drivel." We are "loving" them; but the whole time we are thinking, *Oh, how I would like never to see this person again!* This reveals that we cannot really love God with all our strength unless we first love God with all our mind. In essence, our lifestyle is simply the out-working of our world view, our whole perceptual framework. So, if we are to love God with all our strength, if we are to truly "do the do's and don't the don'ts," we have to love God with all our *mind*.

We begin to try to love God with all our mind. We get all our doctrine worked out, point by point; we get all the i's dotted just right, all the t's crossed just right, all the paragraphs right where they should be. Our biblical understanding is as sound and orthodox as it could possibly be. We attempt to take "every thought captive to obey Christ"

(2 Cor. 10:5, RSV). We even try to have loving thoughts and attitudes toward "the enemy." We get it all worked out, but we discover that, even though we are valiantly trying to love God with all our mind and strength, there surge up from within us feelings, emotions, dynamics that militate against loving God with all our mind and strength. Feelings, desires, impulses about "the enemy" overrule our thoughts, and we "do the don'ts" and lash out at the enemy in some way. We discover that we cannot love God with all our mind and strength until we love God with all our *soul*.

The soul, biblically, has to do with our volitional nature. It can be equated with our will. The dynamics of "soul" are broader, of course, but this is adequate to illustrate our purposes. Have you ever heard, "Persons convinced against their will are of the same opinion still?" This reveals quite accurately how closely the mind is governed by the will, or soul. Another saying is, "Don't confuse me with facts, my mind is made up." This has nothing to do with the mind, it is a matter of the will. I cannot convince you (your mind) of the truth of anything you do not choose to accept as true. You see, our will, or soul, determines the set of our mind which, in turn, determines the course of our action. So, in the case of "the enemy," we seek to "will" to love them. But have you ever noticed when you "will" to do something like this how you tend to do it in your own way, in your own time, in ways which are convenient to your own agenda? It reveals there is still one more level to go. Jesus says we are to love God with all our *heart*.

Let me give you something to meditate on. Take it and work through it for the rest of your life! Here it is: *It is possible for us to will the will of God but not surrender our heart*. I can will the will of God for my life, but I can will to do it in *my* way, at *my* convenience, when it suits *me*, how it suits *me*, in the context that suits *me*. I can honestly and sincerely will to do the will of God without surrendering my heart. This is why there is one more level left after the soul, or will. There is the "me" that wills.

This is why Jesus begins the Great Commandment with

the heart. The heart is the you that is a volitional being, the you that wills. The *first* motion of the will, therefore, in any situation, must be to will the heart to God—not simply willing to do God's will without losing control of ourselves, but willing ourselves to *be God's* in the world. With respect to "the enemy," this means yielding our very being to God *for* "the enemy" and yielding our very being to "the enemy" *for God.* This is what Jesus meant when he spoke of "losing self" for his sake, of denying self, of taking up the cross daily. This is the level at which we relinquish the garbled, distorted, debased word we are and begin to become the word God speaks us forth to be for others.

Our heart-soul level is our state of "being" out of which our "doing"flows. You see, Jesus not only gives us a picture of our spiritual structure in the relationship of heart, soul, mind, and strength. He also reveals the direction of flow in our being. On another occasion Jesus said,

> There is nothing outside of persons which by going into them can defile them; but the things which come out of persons are what defile them. . . . For from within, *out of the heart* of persons, come evil thoughts, fornication, theft, murder, adultery, coveting, wickedness, deceit, licentiousness, envy, slander, pride, foolishness. All these evil things come from within, and they defile a person—Mark 7:15, 21–23.

Our doing ultimately flows from our being. This is why we have such difficulty in "doing the do's and don'ting the don'ts." Whenever our Christian "doing" is a structure imposed from without, it will inevitably be thwarted by the dynamics of being which flow from within. The garbled, distorted, debased word we are within will "shout down" the external imposition of any other word we try to "do."

Spiritual formation is the shaping of our *being.* It is the shaping of our being in the image of Christ, the shaping of our word by the Word of God. Our *doing* is certainly involved in this process, and we will consider this in the next chapter in our full examination of spiritual disciplines.

DYNAMICS OF BIBLICAL EXPERIENCE

Merton gives us six dynamics of biblical experience that help to draw together what we have been considering in the first two sections of this book, and to focus our attention on how these relate to the role of scripture in spiritual formation.

First, he says, "The Bible message is communicated through *happenings* and is implied in the more or less explicit meanings of those happenings, for mankind, for the People of God, for us personally."[1] Merton is speaking here of the inbreaking, intrusive nature of the Word of God into the very midst of life, both the life of humanity through history and our own individual lives.

"Second, these happenings all take on the character of unexpected and free *interventions or breakthroughs*. They are often explosive, astonishing, dramatic." Here is the real point, "They result from a collision of wills. . . . man as an individual or, more often, in his collective and social existence, is determined to achieve some end [the functional, doing mode] which is in conflict with his own inner truth [the relational, being dynamics.]"[2] Merton puts his finger on having our priorities reversed. We are determined to achieve some end (functional, doing) which is in conflict with our *relationship* with God and with the reality of our own *being*. Merton characterizes this as a conflict of wills. This seems to imply that making the informational, functional, doing modes primary in our life is a consequence of our desire to have our own will rather than the will of God. It also suggests the corollary, that seeking the will of God requires that we make the formational, relational, being modes the primary dynamics of our spiritual formation.

Third, "[We] need to be able to listen to other, more inscrutable and more direct commands, issued at the very center of [our] personal existence and reaching into the depths of [our] own identity and freedom in such a way that [we] 'know' they are directly intended for [us] personally by the ultimate Lord of life and death."[3] This reveals the need for the formational, relational dynamics of spiritual formation at the being level and is especially in contrast to the informational mode of "listening" we so habitually practice.

"Fourth, the confrontation of two conflicting freedoms and their interplay in history on two different levels is not static and arbitrary. It is an ongoing relationship which is progressive and formative, and implies historical development of human freedom."[4] We are not slaves, expected to submit blindly to omnipotent power; rather, we are free to respond or not to the freedom of God. This is the nature of covenant relationship. God opens toward us, and we offer ourselves in return. However, this is something that takes place at the *relational* level, not the functional; at the *being* level, not the doing; and the nature of that being in relationship is *formational* not informational.

Fifth, "The New Testament claims to fulfill and to perfect the Abrahamic and Mosaic covenant in a completely new kind of freedom which, according to Paul, demands an emancipation even from the Law."[5] This is an emancipation from the functional, doing dynamic which the Law had become. Being in right relationship with God had become dependent upon and derived from doing what the Law required.

Sixth, "The New Testament asserts that the full manifestation of God is in fact a self-emptying . . . in which God becomes man and even submits to death at the hands of men. . . . The word of God is now not only event but person, and the entire meaning and content of the Bible is to be found . . . not in the message about Christ [informational] but in an encounter with Christ [formational, relational]. . . . To become utterly committed to this person and to share in the event which is his coming, his death, and his resurrection is to find the meaning of existence, not by figuring it out [informational, functional, doing] but by living it as he did [formational, relational, being.]"[6]

Merton then asks,

> *How* is one to share in this event and enter into the Christ-life, how does one participate in the existence of the Son of

Man? . . . Enough to say that the New Testament's answer is "in the word of the cross," by which the shallow self, the ego-self which clings to a relatively superficial and limited freedom centered in its own satisfaction, surrenders to the ultimate Christ-self, the New Man created in justice and holiness of truth . . . in which our freedom is moved not by ego-fantasy but by the Spirit of Christ speaking out of the inmost ground of our being in our encounter with our brother. . . . We reach the peak of freedom and exist entirely *for others*, no longer held back by our own petty limitations. [7]

The "shallow, ego-self" is the life characterized by the primacy of informational, functional, doing dynamics. The "New Man," characterized by the primacy of formational, relational, being dynamics, is a life of kairotic existence, a life shaped by the Word of God, a life that is increasingly the word God speaks it forth to be in the lives of others.

Then, relating this entire matrix of spiritual formation to the role of the scripture, Merton adds, "We cannot enter into this dynamic of freedom and understanding unless, in reading the Bible, we somehow become aware that we are problems to ourselves. The Bible is a message of reconciliation and unity, but in order to awaken us to our need for unity it brings out the contradictions within us and makes us aware of a fundamental division."[8]

If we read the scripture informationally, functionally, at the doing level, it will never have this kind of penetrating, disclosing power in our life. The informational, functional, doing modes inherently insulate us and protect us from the kind of awareness and disclosure Merton is pointing to. We don't like to come face to face with the fact *we* are the problem in the garbled, distorted, debased nature of our word. We don't like to acknowledge the contradictions and fundamental divisions within us. It is only through the disciplined adoption of formational, relational, "being" dynamics in our approach to the scripture that it can become the living Word of God. This Word will penetrate to those depths of our lives where we are a hindrance to what God speaks us forth to be in the world.

Finally, Merton says, "[We close] ourselves in upon the superficial and exterior unity of the emperical ego [the informational, functional, doing mode]. In other words, we affirm our unity on a shallow and provisional level by shutting out other persons and by closing off the deepest area of inner freedom where the ego is no longer in full conscious control."[9] When we do this, we automatically lock ourselves into a primary emphasis upon the informational, functional, doing mode of existence. "Thus, cut off from our true inner selves, we remain alienated beings, *semi-fictions, masks*. Our best energies are wasted in *playing various arbitrary roles*."[10] Here is the functional mode at its most destructive, the doing mode at its most debasing. "Society abets us in this pretence, and does so enthusiastically."[11] This insight is what I have been trying to share with you. When we come to spiritual formation, we are coming up against dynamics of our own being that are manifestations of the sickness of the society of which we are a part. We must be formed in the presence of those things that deform us and garble, distort, and debase the word God speaks us forth to be.

Here we come to the central point of spiritual formation. Our acculturation tends to move us into both perceptual and experiential modes that operate on the principle that all we need for wholeness is simply to bring something more to where we are which will move us to where we want to be. Acquire more information to process, more technique to function with, more "doing" to do, and we will move ourselves into a higher level of wholeness. We tend to look for some piece of information, some technique or method of spiritual formation that will take us from where we are to where we want to be with a minimum of inconvenience, pain, or suffering. We have so emphasized the *Life* dimension of the New Testament that we have avoided coming to grips with its *death* dimension. We have avoided the fact that in the gospel, Life comes out of death, not out of life. Trying to bring Life out of life attempts to escape the necessity of dying to the old parameters of our existence, the necessity of relinquishing the brokenness of

104

our being, the necessity of letting go of those things that warp and misshape and distort who we are. The emphasis upon informational, functional, "doing" dynamics is our attempt to bring Life out of life. But formational, relational, "being" dynamics enable God to lead us to that death from which Life emerges.

I hope you see that if scripture is to become an intrusion of the living Word of God into our lives, if it is to be the point of our being addressed by the Word, if it is to be the place of the transforming encounter with the Word in our life, we need both a radical perceptual shift as well as a deep alteration of our experiential mode of being-doing or function-relation. With all of this now behind us. We are ready to move to consideration of the role of scripture in spiritual formation.

IV.

THE POWER OF SCRIPTURE IN SPIRITUAL FORMATION

10.

Breaking the Crust

---

*A*T last we come to the role of scripture in spiritual formation. We have already touched on several aspects of the scripture in spiritual formation. It is the vehicle of the Word of God which shapes the word God speaks us forth to be in the world. As such, scripture must be approached formationally if it is to become the icon, the opening into Reality, which enables our garbled, distorted, debased word to be drawn into kairotic existence and begin to become the word God speaks us forth to be. Scripture also addresses us most focally at the relational-being level from which our functional-doing dynamics emerge. I hope that some part of this concept has already become ingrained in your perception and experience through what we have been doing. I hope that you already see the role of scripture in your own spiritual formation within completely new parameters, or at least within the possibility of new parameters.

There are three aspects of spiritual formation which I need to share with you before we look specifically at the role of scripture in spiritual formation. The first is "breaking the crust," the second is spiritual discipline, and the third is nurturing growth.

BREAKING THE CRUST

The first aspect of spiritual formation is what I call "breaking the crust." George MacDonald, that great Scottish novelist, poet, and Christian writer who was so instrumental in the conversion of C. S. Lewis, wrote in *Diary of and Old Soul:*

> With every morn my life afresh must break
> The crust of self, gathered about me fresh;
> That thy wind-spirit may rush in and shake
> The darkness out of me, and rend the mesh
> The spider-devils spin out of the flesh—
> Eager to net the soul before it wake,
> That it may slumberous lie, and listen to the snake.[1]

We build, maintain, and defend a complex structure of habits, attitudes, and perceptions, of dynamics of personal and corporate relationships, and of patterns of reaction and response to the world. This complex structure enables us to cope with life. But this structure also becomes an ever-thickening crust of self that imprisons and limits us. It garbles, distorts, and debases that word that God is speaking us forth to be. It prevents our growth into wholeness. It thwarts our shaping by the living Word of God.

It is the reality of this "crust of self" that has required our lengthy focus on the perceptual and experiential dynamics ingrained in us by our culture. Those perceptual and experiential elements are the primary dynamics of the crust of self. If our view of ourselves is anything less than being a word spoken forth by God, then our self image is a self-constructed facade—a crust of self. This self finds itself required to hold the world at arm's length and manipulate it through the use of informational and functional dynamics in order to maintain the facade, rather than being open and receptive to the shaping and transforming presence of God who meets it in the world. This self approaches the scripture informationally and utilizes it functionally to support and maintain the facade rather than being open

110

and receptive to the living, penetrating Word of God who meets it in the scripture. This self lives in a world of its own making in which its "doings" are all designed to maintain and control the facade, rather than being open and receptive to God's new order of being in Christ which is the matrix of true self and wholeness. The crust of self is developed, maintained, and protected by the informational, functional, doing modes that prevail in our culture and in our lives. These dynamics are particularly well-suited for enabling us to deal with life on our own terms. Their use facilitates our regulation and control of life in our own way.

I have come to realize that the primary work of God's grace in our lives is to liberate us from this destructive bondage to the crust of self in order to shape us into wholeness. God is seeking to create in us a whole new structure of habits, attitudes, and perceptions, of dynamics of personal and corporate relationships, of patterns of reaction and response to the world. This new structure is one of increasing Christlikeness. God is seeking to break the crust.

We have already considered the biblical alternatives to the crust of self. We have discovered that we are a word spoken forth by God into the world. We have discovered that our word is shaped into wholeness by the living Word of God. We have discovered that the living Word of God encounters us particularly in the scripture. We have seen that scripture is iconographic: it opens windows of perception and experience into God's new order of being in Christ—kairotic existence. All of these biblical alternatives help to break the crust of self. We have also considered the operational dynamics of the crust of self. We have discovered that the relational, formational, being dynamics set forth in the Bible militate against the garbling, distorting, debasing destructiveness of the informational, functional, doing focus by which the crust of self seeks to maintain and defend its facade.

The core of spiritual formation is the process of breaking the crust of self and bringing forth a new creation in the image of Christ—breaking the garbled, debased, distorted word we have become, and bringing forth the word God speaks us forth to be in the world. The focal question is:

How? How are we to break the crust? Or, more accurately, how are we to allow God to break the crust? How are we to be conformed to the image of Christ? What is our responsibility in this process and what is God's? The answer is the second point we must consider in spiritual formation—spiritual discipline.

SPIRITUAL DISCIPLINES

Spiritual discipline is one of the essential rhythms of kairotic existence. I hope that there has been a shift in both your perceptual and experiential dynamics toward spiritual formation. I am not expecting you to have successfully processed everything thus far. But I hope you realize now that spiritual formation has something to do with the formation rather than the information mode, that spiritual formation is a means of formation by the Word of God rather than a means of information by which we can make changes in ourselves. I hope you see that spiritual formation is relational or "being" oriented rather than functional or "doing" oriented. Spiritual formation is a dynamic of relationship with God which shapes our being rather than a technique or method or program for self-improvement.

Within spiritual formation, a spiritual discipline is something we offer to God as a means of God's grace in our lives. It is an act of loving obedience offered to God to be used for *God's* purposes in our lives. What this means is that *anything* and *everything* we do can be a spiritual discipline *if* we offer it to God as a means for God to use in our lives if he so chooses. This is the way that "doing" becomes "being," when we offer our "doing" to God and keep offering it and keep offering it as a means for God to do whatever he wants to do. This releases what we are doing from being functional because no longer is it something *we* are doing to try to make ourselves better or to impress God or others. It becomes a spiritual discipline. It becomes something we offer up to God to be used as God wishes.

Let me give you a litmus test to determine if you are engaging in a spiritual discipline. Are you willing to offer something to God as a discipline and to keep offering it day after day, week after week, month after month, year after year—to continue offering it for God to use in whatever way he wants in your life and *have God do absolutely nothing with it?* If you are (and don't answer that too quickly!), then you are engaging in a spiritual discipline that will cut to the heart of all of those dynamics of our culture that tend to misshape our formation.

Another detrimental aspect of our culture, which we noted briefly in chapter 3, is its stress upon instant gratification. We want instant return on our investments. We put our quarter into the machine, and we expect our candy bar at the bottom before the sound of the coin fades away. If it doesn't get there fast enough, we start pounding on the machine. How often we do the same thing, figuratively, in our spiritual disciplines! We put our discipline into the slot, and we expect an instant blessing to come forth. If it doesn't come immediately, we start "pounding" on God. We remind God of his responsibility in the face of our "faithfulness." We demand God's response because we have done our part in performing the "discipline." When there is no response, we drop the "discipline;" we try another "discipline;" we find another person, group, or book to be our spiritual mentor, all in a vain attempt to get an instant return on our spiritual investment.

Spiritual disciplines must take place within a Christian community, a fact we noted in our discussion of community as a rhythm of kairotic existence. We need the support and encouragement, even the loving correction or chastisement of our sisters and brothers in Christ. They help us maintain our spiritual disciplines in the face of personal dynamics that militate against our spiritual disciplines. Another reason for the necessity of a spiritual guide or a spiritual formation group is because there are disciplines we offer up to God which may not be the disciplines God would have us offer. As noted in chapter 7, we tend to adopt spiritual disciplines that allow us to remain pretty much as we are. Frequently, we are not in a position to be able to discern this for ourselves. We need the wisdom of a spiritual guide or of a group of brothers and sisters in the Lord who are open, responsive, receptive, and loving enough to be an instrument of God for us.

Now, this raises the question: Can there be a wrong spiritual discipline or a bad spiritual discipline? In one sense, anything can be a spiritual discipline. In fact, if you offer something to God consistently, day by day, and keep offering it, and God chooses not to use it, that could be one of your most profound points of real spiritual formation. It is a formation in unconditional trust. If God chooses not to use it, you praise God and continue to offer it for his non-use. You are not making demands on God. You are yielding yourself to allow God to do what is desired.

Even if you should offer to God a discipline which may not be exactly what is expected, God will honor it if it is genuinely offered, if you are not trying to manipulate God. However, God may also lead you away from that inappropriate discipline into the discipline that is intended for you. The key to the whole situation is whether or not we are truly releasing ourselves and the discipline to God for his use.

The reading of scripture is a spiritual discipline. One of the problems we have, however, is that when our reading of scripture becomes dry and doesn't seem to "do" anything for us any more, our tendency is to look somewhere else. We look to the "Christian top ten" reading list, or the latest "bright light" in Christian literature. Now, it could be that what I have been sharing with you has opened up new vistas and new ways for the scripture to become the Word of God in your life. But there is also the need to be willing to wait upon the Word. There is the necessity of offering our reading of the scripture up to God to be used as God chooses and when God chooses.

For example, take my experience where God finally said, "You are Pharaoh." That period of scripture reading had been *dry!* I was reading through Exodus and it was even less than informational. I already knew it practically by heart. I was mostly going through the motions. But I *was* seeking to be faithful; I was seeking to be open; I was seeking to be receptive. Then, finally, the Word came. Part of

114

the reason that it took so long may be because, deep down inside, I was hearing and immediately closing off my inner ears to what God was saying. I didn't want that kind of identification. I didn't want to face up to the necessity of that kind of dying.

There are still passages I sit before again and again and again, awaiting the Word, and as yet, it has not come. My suspicion is that there may be passages in which this will be the case until the end of my life. There are others where I am beginning to sense that I am not yet ready for the Word. God has some deep cleansing and forming work to do before I can come to the point of hearing the Word in those passages. But the secret is to keep coming back to those passages to sit before them in receptivity, and to listen. Even when we don't hear anything, just the act of adopting that posture is spiritually forming. It is opening us to the deep work of God's grace which will bring us to the point of being able to be addressed by the living Word.

Susan Muto, writing of spiritual reading as a discipline, says that the person engaged in this way, "is solely intent on pleasing God without demanding returns for his dedication and fidelity. Such inner purification of motive and desire prepares the way for a deepening intimacy through grace which is beyond our perception."[2] This is the relinquishment of spiritual discipline, especially the spiritual discipline of reading the scripture. We release ourselves to let God do what God wants to do.

In his covenant prayer,[3] John Wesley gives a very powerful focus to this essential posture of yieldedness: "I will be no longer my own, but give up myself to thy will in all things. . . . Let me be employed for Thee." Here that old functional mode of ours just bubbles up to the surface and off we go. We want to be busy, active, effective workers for the Lord. But the other half of it is: ". . . or laid aside for Thee." And we have trouble with that. "Let me be full." Sure! "Let me be empty." *Huh?* "Let me have all things." Yes! "Let me have nothing." *What?* We can very easily pray the first parts of the covenant prayer, but the other sides are much more difficult for us. Wesley is putting his finger on the necessity of relinquishment. This is the key to genuine spiritual discipline and the heart of our approach to the scripture in spiritual formation.

NURTURING GROWTH

If breaking the crust and spiritual discipline are two facets of spiritual formation, the third is nurturing our growth into wholeness. God's grace liberates us from bondage to the crust of self. Genuine spiritual disciplines then allow our word to be shaped by the living Word of God.

This leads us into some of the "how" questions we will be looking at in the last chapters. But here we also encounter the problem between the functional and the relational, perhaps at the deepest level. We want the answer to the question, "How does the Word nurture me into wholeness?" Subtly contained within that question is the question, "What do I have to do?" The functional-doing mode is slipping in here when we are not looking.

Paul reminds us, "We are his workmanship" (Eph. 2:10, RSV). If we offer genuine spiritual disciplines with the intention of allowing God to do through them whatever God wants, to break the crust of our self in whatever way God wants, to nurture us in whatever way God wants, then there is a necessity of letting *God* do it and not trying to take the control back to ourselves.

The basic way in which the Word nurtures our growth is by obedience. The secret of nurture however, is that our obedience must also be offered to God as a spiritual discipline. Obedience is not something I am doing to shape myself in God's image, but an obedience to the Word which I also offer up that God may use it to shape me by grace. We are addressed by the Word. We then obey. We offer to God some specific act of obedience to God's Word at a point in our life *where what we are in our being is not in harmony with that act of obedience;* at a point where our "doing" does not flow from our "being." When we consistently offer ourselves to God in this act of obedience as a true spiritual discipline—not demanding or predetermining or attaching our own agendas to the discipline, but of-

116

fering it solely as a means of grace for God's use—then, in God's timing, we make a discovery. God has worked in our being through the Holy Spirit to transform what we are so that the obedience we "do" becomes the outflow of our "being." We have, at that point, become the word God speaks us forth to be.

This is where the functional and the relational flow together in holistic spiritual formation. However, there is always the temptation to view your obedience as functional. You are tempted to say, "Well now, Lord, I've obeyed; now I expect something in return." This is subtle; it sneaks up on you. You constantly have to allow *that* crust of self to be broken, too. Another temptation is to think, "Okay, I'll do this, and that will change me; then I'll have the result." But in genuine spiritual formation the *nature* of the doing is the secret.

Paul sets forth the transforming dynamic of spiritual formation in a beautiful illustration in Colossians 1:9–10, where he prays that the Colossians, "might be filled with *the knowledge of his will*." Paul's word for "knowledge" here is an intensified kind of knowledge. It is not cognitive-informational only. It includes that, but it is also experiential knowledge. It is the experience of being penetrated by the living Word of God; it is the experience of being addressed.

Paul then prays, "That you may be filled with the knowledge of his will *to walk worthily of him*, fully pleasing to him, bearing fruit in every good work." The purpose of the encounter with the will of God is obedience. Finally, Paul indicates the outcome of all this, "that you might increase in *the knowledge of God*." Thus Paul sketches the dynamic of spiritual formation from encounter with the will of God, to obedience to God's will, to "knowledge" of God. Again, as with knowledge of God's will, this is an experiential-relational knowledge. It is having our being conformed to God's image. Our life in God's will is then no longer a matter of an obedience we offer to God as a means of grace; it becomes the fabric of our being. We discover that God uses the disciplines we offer as means of grace in order to nurture in us a new structure of habits, attitudes, perceptions, of dynamics of personal and corporate relationships, and of patterns of reaction and response to the world. God creates in us a new structure of being which is conformed to the image of Christ. We become the word God speaks us forth to be.

An important aspect of this mode of nurturing growth is that we don't wait until we are perfect before we do what God wants us to do. We acknowledge that very often what we are doing is garbled and distorted by our own inadequacies and incompleteness; by the old structures of habit, attitude, and perception; by the old dynamics of relationship; by the old patterns of reaction and response. However, if we are seeking deeper and deeper obedience to God as we move forward, if we offer it all to God as a means of grace in our lives, God can redeem our mistakes. God does not expect perfection of action, but perfection of intention—the offering of our obedience.

Whatever role scripture has in our spiritual formation, its role must be inseparably conjoined with the essential elements of spiritual formation: breaking the crust, spiritual disciplines, and nurturing growth. These three elements are the heartbeat of vital Christian spirituality. Without a breaking of the crust of self, we remain imprisoned by the old structure of habits, attitudes, and perceptions; by the old dynamics of personal and corporate relationships; and by the old patterns of reaction and response to the world. Without genuine spiritual disciplines which open us to the transforming power of God's work in our inner being, our attempts at spiritual life and growth are merely manipulative, functional attempts either to maintain and defend the old structure of our being or to restructure it according to our own purposes. Without breaking the crust and genuine spiritual disciplines, there can be no experience of God's nurturing growth into a new structure of being. As we have begun to see, and we will see more fully, scripture plays a vital role in these essential elements of spiritual formation.

118

11.

Wesley's Guidelines for Reading Scripture

*A*S we now begin to look at specific, practical, methodological aspects of the role of scripture in spiritual formation, let us once again open ourselves and give God permission to use this time we have together:

Our Father, we thank you that you have been touching our lives: illuminating us; opening us at deep levels of our being; stretching us at points of our narrowness; confronting us where we are garbled, distorted, and debased; challenging us to become the word you speak us forth to be; but in every way working in it all for your good purposes in our lives. As we begin to consider ways of coming to scripture which will enable it to become your living Word in our lives, help us, O Lord, to remain open to the guidance of your Holy Spirit. Amen.

John Wesley's guidelines for reading scripture are an excellent description of the posture that is necessary if our reading is to become an encounter with the living, penetrating Word of God. Wesley's guidelines move us from the informational to the formational level of reading, from the functional to the relational dynamic of response to what we read, and from the "doing" to the "being" mode of implementation of what we read.

In introducing his guidelines Wesley says:

> This is the way to understand [informational] the things of God: "Meditate thereon day and night;" so shall you attain the best knowledge, even to "know the only true God, and Jesus Christ whom He hath sent" [formational/relational]. And this knowledge will lead you "to love Him, because He hath first loved us;" yea, "to love the Lord your God with all your heart, and with all your soul, and with all your mind, and with all your strength" [relational/being]. . . . And in consequence of this, while you joyfully experience all the holy tempers described in this book [being], you will likewise be outwardly "holy as He that hath called you is holy, in all manner of conversation" [doing which flows from being].[1]

Wesley is here speaking of a process of approaching scripture that opens us to the living Word. This approach leads us into spiritual disciplines through which God can break the crust of self which garbles, distorts, and debases us, and which results in the nurture of the Word that enables us to be the word God speaks us forth to be in the world.

TIME

If we desire to read scripture in such a way that we become, through the shaping of the Word, the word God speaks us forth to be, the first thing Wesley tells us is, "To set apart a little time, if you can, every morning and evening for that purpose." I hear Wesley saying two things in this first guideline, which I would commend to you for your own use of scripture in your spiritual formation.

First, our use of scripture in spiritual formation must be a regular, consistent, daily feeding upon the Word; it must be a spiritual discipline as defined in chapter 10. We are to undertake reading scripture as a regular, consistent discipline, an action, a "function," something we "do;" but we offer it up to God as a means of grace so our reading can become formational, relational. This offering is, as we have seen, the heart, the core, the inner dynamic of spiritual discipline. But then, there is also the regularity of the discipline, the persistent, daily sticking with it.

Second, in the words "set apart," I hear Wesley saying there needs to be not only a disciplined, daily time of reading the scripture, but an unhindered time. The idea of unhindered time has two implications.

One, it needs to be *outwardly* unhindered. You need, if at all possible, to have a time when you will not have interruptions or disruptions of your reading, to have a time when there will not be outside intrusions into your opening of yourself to the Word. For some, this may be impossible, especially at certain stages of life. But it should be the goal toward which we move in establishing our set apart time.

Two, the set apart time needs to be *inwardly* unhindered. It needs to be a time where you can let go of the pressures, the problems, the burdens of your daily life for that period of time. It should be a time where you can center down or be still and be open to God alone, a time when you can be in the presence of God's Word. There needs to be an inner as well as an outer solitude, inner as well as outer silence. This, too, may be impossible for some, but it should be the ideal we seek in setting apart a time for the scripture.

One additional aspect of this set apart time is to give God your best possible time. Often, we give God the "left over" time, when all the other responsibilities of our lives have been met. We come to God with our energies depleted, our emotions at low ebb, our minds dulled by the duties of the day, our spirits sluggish. Is it any wonder that we so infrequently encounter the living Word in our reading of scripture? or that our discipline of scripture reading becomes irregular and haphazard? We need to give God our best time, the time when we are alert, sensitive, fully alive, responsive. For many, this time is at the beginning of the day; for others, it is some point during the day or in the evening. Whatever that point is for you, that is when you should set apart time for reading the scripture. You should give God that part of your day when your attention and alertness are at their peak, the time when you can be "fully there." Here too, of course, it will not always be possible to do this at all stages of our life, but we should seek to give God the best possible time.

BALANCE

Wesley's second instruction is, "At each time, if you have leisure, read a chapter out of the Old and one out of the New Testament; if you cannot do this, take a single chapter, or a part of one." There are at least three things implied in what Wesley is saying.

First, he is talking about an ordered discipline, an orderly working through the whole of scripture. As Christians, we have a strong tendency to focus our reading on the New Testament. We often tend to think of the Old Testament as second class scripture. I hope that this is not true for you; but if it is, then Wesley is reminding you that there needs to be a balance in your reading of scripture. We need to read in both the Old and the New Testament.

Second, another tendency in our use of scripture in spiritual formation is to keep returning to those passages that have nurtured us in the past. We all have certain passages that have been deeply enriching for us, passages in which we have been addressed by God, passages where we have been shaped by the Word. We tend to gravitate to these passages with a much higher frequency than we move to new areas of the scripture. As in our physical nature, if we eat only one kind of food persistently and do not have a balanced diet, we begin to experience deterioration. The same is true spiritually. Part of the structure of a holistic spiritual discipline of scripture reading is to have some means by which we work through the whole of scripture. One way to do this is to use a lectionary.[2] A lectionary usually gives you an Old Testament reading, an Epistle reading, and a Gospel reading. Over a period of two, three, or more years, a lectionary will move you through the entire Bible.

Third, Wesley seems to be indicating that we should work with fairly small units. We are reading for formation,

not information. Here is where the lectionary is also bene-
ficial. It preselects the amounts for you, usually a rather
brief portion. Often, I find that I want to move beyond
what the lectionary "allows." I become interested in the
"story" and want to cover it all as quickly as possible—the
informational dynamics tend to take over. However, if I am
faithful to the discipline of the lectionary, I am forced to
stop and move more deeply into the passage at hand; I am
required to still myself before the text and seek to allow the
Word to address me out of that portion before me. The fact
that Wesley is perfectly comfortable with reading only a
portion of a chapter seems to indicate that he is thinking in
terms of formational reading rather than informational.

FOCAL INTENTION

Once you have developed a means of working through
scripture in a balanced and formational way, Wesley says
that you should approach each passage "with a single eye,
to know the whole will of God, and a fixed resolution to do
it." This is the heart of the approach to scripture in spiritual
formation.

First, Wesley says the intention of our reading should be
to know the whole will of God. We should come to the
scripture with the focal purpose of encountering the will of
God for our life. We should come in openness to what God
wants for us at every level of our being, in every facet of our
relationships, in all of our activities and involvements. To
read the scripture in this way is to bring the whole of our
life before God and to expectantly and receptively seek
God's will for everything in our living. We come with our
habits, attitudes, and perspectives; we come with our dynamics of personal and corporate relationships; we come
with our patterns of reaction and response to the world
around us; and we seek for God to speak the Word into our
lives in any or all of these areas. We come with our "crust of
self;" we come with our garbled, distorted, debased
"word;" and we seek to be addressed by the living Word,
which can make us whole.

Second, Wesley says we should seek the whole will of

God with a *fixed resolution to do it!* Here is the key of our approach to scripture. Often students come to me wrestling with something in their lives. They are working through a series of complex responsibilities, options, and desires, trying to discern God's will for their lives in the midst of their situation. The question I always ask them, in one form or other, is, "Are you ready to *do* God's will in this situation, *no matter what God's will may be?*" They usually say yes. Then I begin to probe them at this point, because I have discovered that my tendency is to say to the Lord, "What is Your will?" Then I can set God's will up against all the rest of my options and pick what *I* think is best. I have also discovered that when this is the mode in which I seek God's will, it is amazing how closed the heavens are.

A beautiful illustration of the fixed intent to do God's will is found in Exodus 19:3–8. Moses goes up to God on Mt. Sinai and the Lord says to him,

> Thus you shall say to the house of Jacob, and tell the people of Israel: You have seen what I did to the Egyptians, and how I bore you on eagle's wings and brought you to myself. Now therefore, if you will obey my voice and keep my covenant, you shall be my own possession among all the peoples; for all the earth is mine, and you shall be to me a kingdom of priests and a holy nation. These are the words which you shall speak to the children of Israel (RSV).

Moses goes down the mountain, calls the elders together, and tells them all that the Lord had said. Between 19:7 and 8, we must presume the elders went and told the people and received their response; for in 19:8, the people respond, "All that the Lord has spoken we will do" (RSV). But what has the Lord spoken? Nothing, not one single command, not one single statute, not one single ordinance; all God has said is if they will obey, he will be their God and they will be God's people. This is a calling for their unconditional obedience to God's will, a "fixed resolution to do it" *when* it is revealed *before* it is revealed. This is what Wes-

124

ley is talking about in the third step: to read the scripture, to open your life to that living Word of God, to know God's Word spoken to your life *in order to do it*. This is one of the crucial dynamics for moving from informational to formational reading: an inner decision, down in the center of your being, that whatever God speaks into your life you are going to do.

HOLISTIC REALITY

Wesley then says, "Have a constant eye to the analogy of faith, the connection and harmony there is between those grand fundamental doctrines, original sin, justification by faith, the new birth, inward and outward holiness." We must realize that in the scripture we are not dealing with isolated pieces that are somehow hermetically sealed from one another. We are dealing with a great, holistic unity. We are dealing with the living reality of God's purpose, power, and presence in our lives and in our world. To put this into terms we have developed, Wesley is saying that everything that addresses us out of the scripture relates in some way to kairotic existence, to God's new order of being in Christ. It may be a Word of God that reveals some brokenness or disobedience in our lives, some dynamic of sin. It may be a Word that offers us God's grace, love, and forgiveness for that brokenness and disobedience. It may be a Word that awakens us to the possibility of a new life at that point. It may be a Word that calls us, at that point in our lives, to a total consecration to God (inner holiness) and to a new life of consistent obedience in the world (outer holiness). These are the focal areas of our lives that the living Word addresses and penetrates.

This is part of what Paul was saying when he wrote: "Fully appropriate for yourselves the *kairos*" (Eph. 5:16). We must be very careful not to fall into the trap of "cubby holing" the Word of God into nice, neat, objective, systematic categories. Such activity represents the informational/ functional dynamic. We must realize that in reading the scripture we are engaged with a living and holistic Reality, Who seeks to form our lives into wholeness of being and doing.

125

PRAYERFUL READING

The fifth thing Wesley says about approaching the scripture is that "serious and earnest prayer should be consistently used before we consult the oracles of God; seeing 'Scripture can only be understood through the same Spirit whereby it was given.' Our reading should likewise be closed with prayer, that what we read may be written on our hearts." Wesley here places the emphasis upon the relational rather then the functional dynamic. We should enter into scripture in the relational mode; we should open ourselves to God in prayer at the deeper levels of our being. This is prayer that opens us to the Spirit who brought that scripture into being in the first place; the same Spirit who is now at work in our reading to make that scripture the living Word of God that addresses us.

Here we encounter the "dynamic of inspiration" involved in the scripture. The inspiration of the scripture involves you and me as much as the original writer, together with the whole process in the church, under the guidance of the Spirit, which brought the scripture writings into an authoritative collection—the canon. In prayerful, relational/formational reading of the scripture, we become participants in the process of inspiration. This is what I hear Wesley saying here. Prayerful reading of scripture is the opening of ourselves to that order of being, that kairotic existence, out of which scripture speaks to us and forms our life in Christ.

ADDRESS AND RESPONSE

Finally, Wesley says, "It might also be of use [he is a master of understatement!] if, while we read, we were frequently to pause and examine ourselves by what we read, both with regard to our heart and lives." This is the conscious, disciplined opening of ourselves to be addressed by the Word. It is, on the one hand, the examination of the outer actions of our lives. What is going on in our personal and corporate relationships? What is taking place in our patterns of reaction and response? What is happening at work, at home, in the church, in our social activities? What is occuring in all the outer situations of our life? It is, on the other hand, the examination of the inner dynamics of our being. What is going on in our attitudes, our habits, our feelings, our emotions? What is taking place in our perceptions, our motives? In all these things, the inner (heart) and outer (lives), we open ourselves to God; we bring them before the Word; we let them sink down before the Word and be addressed by God.

Wesley suggests we pause "frequently" for this examination of our inner being and outer doing, a primary aspect of formational reading. Rather than trying to cover a certain amount of scripture, we seek to allow the text to draw us into its depths. Instead of informing the text with our own agenda, we bring the inner and outer dynamics of our life to be formed by the text. Instead of trying to bring the text under our control, we allow the text to take control of our being and doing. This is the discipline of allowing a portion of the text to become iconographic, of stilling ourselves before the kairotic dimensions of the text, and allowing the Word to probe and penetrate both our being and our doing.

Then Wesley adds, "Whatever light you then receive should be used to the uttermost, and that immediately. Let there be no delay. Whatever you resolve begin to execute the first moment you can." Here we come to the point of immediate obedience to the Word that has addressed us. This is where the spiritual discipline of reading scripture leads us into the spiritual discipline of offering to God our loving obedience to God's Word at very particular points of our lives. At some very particular point, the Word speaks to our garbled, distorted, debased "word." As we steadily offer to God the spiritual discipline of obedience *at that very point*, God graciously works through that discipline to transform our very being into the word He speaks us forth to be.

In stressing the "uttermost," the "immediate," the "undelayed" obedience to the Word that has illumined us, Wesley implies the fulfillment of his third guideline—the *fixed intent* to do God's will. If we find ourselves equivocating, rationalizing, justifying our lack of obedience, then we need to back up to step three and examine our hearts before the Lord at that point. How sincere am I here? Am I seeking the *whole* will of God for my life? Do I want the living Word to probe and penetrate *any* and *all* areas of my being and doing? Do I really have a *fixed intent* to obey?

Now there will be those times when, at step three, you truly have no doubts about your sincerity. You truly want to be addressed by the Word. You honestly want to hear what God has to say to you. But then what you hear goes so much deeper into your life than you expected! Up to a certain level you were, with absolute integrity, willing to obey. But now you find the Word pushes you up against the limits of your willingness. You may have been willing to do the will of God, but on your own terms, in your own way, at your own convenience. Now the Word calls you to will your heart completely. Frequently, you may find your spiritual discipline of reading scripture will keep moving you from step six to step three until your "fixed intent" is at the level of total consecration to the will of God, *whatever it may be*.

Wesley's guidelines for reading scripture, as amplified here, provide for us an approach to scripture in spiritual formation. If consistently practiced, these guidelines will enable us to read scripture formationally and relationally. The dynamics of these guidelines will allow the scriptures to become iconographic. Using these guidelines will draw us into those dimensions of kairotic existence through which God can transform our garbled, debased, distorted word into the word God speaks us forth to be in the world. By this process, the scripture becomes the means of grace by which God shapes our lives.

12

Obstacles to Spiritual Reading

A S you begin reading scripture as a spiritual discipline, you will encounter a number of obstacles to your spiritual reading. The most important of these obstacles, the perceptual and experiential dynamics of our culture which are deeply ingrained in our being and doing, have been extensively discussed in the second and third sections of this book. Perhaps it will be helpful if we summarize those general and programmatic obstacles first before looking at some of the specific and particular obstacles to spiritual reading.

PERCEPTUAL OBSTACLES

There are four major perceptual obstacles to which we must always be alert in our spiritual reading: our self image, our perception of reading, our view of the Bible, and our perception of existence.

First, our self image. If we fail to see ourselves as a word spoken forth by God, even though garbled, distorted, and debased, then our spiritual reading will fall under a self image characterized by self-generated, self-maintained, self-directed, and self-protective dynamics. With this kind of self image, we will have a strong tendency to read the scripture in ways that only serve to confirm our false self image. Unless we are at least open to the possibility of being a word spoken forth by God, our reading of scripture will only produce echoes of our self image which then serve to confirm and strengthen that self image. This is a formidable obstacle to our spiritual reading of scripture.

One of the best ways to overcome this obstacle is to infuse each period of spiritual reading of the scripture with the constant and conscious reminder that you are a word spoken forth by God. Remember that God is seeking to shape your word by the Word as you open yourself to God in the scripture. You must nurture a deep desire for God to take what you are and make you what he wants you to be.

Second, our perception of reading. If we fail to come to the scripture formationally, then the informational dynamics of reading that have so shaped our lives will exert their control. We will find ourselves holding the scripture at arm's length and dealing manipulatively with the text in an objective, analytical manner which will reflect back to us our own conscious or unconscious agendas. We will find ourselves dealing with the surface of the text, rather than its depths; substituting quantity of reading for quality; addressing the text rather than being addressed by it; seeking to exercise our control over the text rather than allowing it to have control over us. Even if we have successfully overcome the first obstacle and come to the scripture seeking for God to speak us forth through His Word, informational reading will tend to bring forth what we *think* or *hope* God is speaking us forth to be rather than bringing us into a penetrating and probing encounter with the living Word of God that will begin to shape us as the word God speaks us forth to be.

The best way to overcome this obstacle is by coming to the spiritual reading of scripture with a perception that yields control of the process to the text. Consciously submit yourself to the text, wait before it in receptivity, quieten your own agenda, and listen for the Word to address you. A close attendance to Wesley's guidelines, a conscious attention to the dynamics of formational reading, and the

130

use of techniques of spiritual reading to be set forth in the next chapter are the best means for entering into this mode of spiritual reading.

Third, our view of the Bible. If we fail to understand the iconographic nature of the Bible, then we will see it as a collection of pictures, images, myths, and ideas which we interpret, analyze, demythologize, and categorize according to our own understandings and perceptions. This obstacle is an inseparable companion to the one we have just discussed—informational reading. No matter how consciously and consistently we seek to come to the scripture in a formational mode of reading, unless we also have an awareness of the iconographic nature of the Bible, we will be forced to resort to informational dynamics to process the material we encounter. Unless we perceive the text as a "window" that draws us into the realm of the living Word of God, unless we view the scripture as an icon that draws us into a different order of being where our garbled, distorted, debased "word" is confronted by the Word of God, we will only apply what we read from within the parameters of our old realm of being.

The best way to overcome this obstacle is to remind ourselves constantly of the iconographic nature of the Bible. We should come to the scripture expectantly, receptively, openly, eagerly waiting for God to breathe the living Word in and through the icons into our life. Some of the techniques of spiritual reading in the next chapter will assist you in this process and facilitate your victory over this obstacle.

Fourth, our perception of existence. If we come to the scripture with no perception of the reality of kairotic existence, no awareness of God's radical new order of being in Christ, then our activity will be fruitless. Our spiritual reading of scripture will result in little more than a tinkering with our present system of values, a rearrangement of our present structures of life, a modification of our present dynamics of being and doing. If we have no appreciation of an alternate order of being to the one in which we find ourselves imprisoned and by which our "word" is garbled, debased and distorted, then we can expect little change.

Our only option is to hope to find something in the scripture that will redesign aspects of the old order in ways more suitable to us. This, of course, throws us into the informational, functional, doing modes; locks us into our old, self-generated self image; removes the iconographic possibilities of scripture.

This obstacle may be ultimately overcome by the dawning awareness of the reality of kairotic existence in our own experience. If this has not yet been your experience, then you can begin by being open to the possibility of a genuinely new and radically alternative order of being standing behind the Bible. You can approach the scripture "as if" there is a vitally transforming realm of being that forms the deep matrix of the biblical story and presses for release in your life through the scripture.

As you have undoubtedly realized, these four obstacles are powerfully interrelated. Our self image largely determines the mode in which we approach our reading of scripture. A self-generated self image will, of necessity, utilize an informational approach to protect and maintain its existence against anything that appears to be a threat. The informational approach will have extreme difficulty in viewing the Bible iconographically; indeed, it cannot, for to do so would move it into the formational mode. If the Bible is not viewed iconographically, then the possibility of kairotic existence, a radical alternative to the present order of being, becomes extremely difficult to perceive. Without a perception (and consequently an experience) of kairotic existence, we find ourselves locked into a self image that can only make cosmetic changes in its value system, its structure of activities, and its dynamics of being and doing since it is limited by its present order of being.

EXPERIENTIAL OBSTACLES

There are two experiential obstacles to spiritual reading to which we must also be alert: functional and "doing" dynamics.

First, functional dynamics. If we come to the spiritual reading of scripture in the functional mode, entering into the activity as a means to accomplish our own agenda in our own way and in our own strength, then we will manipulate the scripture for the fulfillment of our agenda. The scripture will simply become a tool of our purposes, our desires, and our needs. This will be particularly destructive if, in our functional approach, we employ what we are doing as a manipulation of God, or, perhaps even worse, as a purportedly "God endorsed" manipulation of ourselves or others.

The antidote to this obstacle is, of course, the relational approach to spiritual reading. We enter into the discipline not for the purpose of promoting our own agenda, but to allow God's "agenda" to come to bear upon our lives. Here again, a diligent application of Wesley's guidelines and the techniques in the next chapter will assist you in overcoming this obstacle.

Second, "doing" dynamics. If we enter into the discipline of spiritual reading with the idea that what we are doing will, *in and of itself*, make us what we think God wants us to be, then we will be constructing a facade of activity which we and others will tend to mistake for genuine spirituality. The scripture will tend to become a source for our ever-expanding list of "do's and don'ts," while what we are in our inner being will be further garbled, distorted, and debased, untouched by all our diligent and frenetic "doing."

The solution to this obstacle is, as we have noted, the practice of genuine spiritual discipline. We must offer our discipline of spiritual reading to God, with no strings attached, no demands, no limits, no expectations. We must offer it to God for his purposes, allowing it to become a means of God's grace to transform our being.

Not only are these two experiential obstacles interrelated, they are also inseparably linked with the perceptual obstacles to spiritual reading. The experiential dynamics are the action side of our perceptual dynamics, the lifestyle of our world view. Thus these perceptual/experiential obstacles to spiritual reading require that we come to the scripture with a conscious, consistent, disciplined adoption of an alternative perceptual/experiential mode such as has been set forth in the second and third sections of this book. Wesley's guidelines, together with the techniques suggested in the next chapter, will greatly facilitate your adoption of such an alternative mode of reading the scripture.

PARTICULAR OBSTACLES

One of the more specific obstacles encountered in spiritual reading is lack of attention. You seek to still yourself, to be open to the Word. You read the text, you reread it, you reread it, and all of a sudden you discover you are thinking about last night's television show or the meeting coming up tomorrow or the children who need braces on their teeth. Life intrudes. You realize you are sitting there and your eyes are going through the motions of running over the words on the page, but your being is somewhere else.

Don't fight this experience, it will just make it stronger. Instead, calmly, steadily, gently, but persistently return to the text. Start again to still and open yourself before the text and bring your attention to focus upon the passage before you. If you again find yourself going off in another direction, just firmly return to the text and begin reading again. As often as distractions intrude or your attention wanders, return to the text, to opening yourself to God, and to being still before the Word. If you keep doing this, gradually you will develop the ability to still yourself before the Word and to "be there" with God.

There will always be times in your life when, because of the circumstances of your life and the kinds of pressures that can sometimes build up beyond the bearing point, these kinds of distractions and intrustions will become major obstacles to your spiritual reading. But with a steady and persistent discipline offered to God, you can experience an increasingly established ability to center down, to be still before the Word, and to be attentively present to God. Whenever distractions come, don't let them throw you off balance, don't worry about them, just return to the text. This is one of the beauties of the spiritual discipline of reading scripture; it gives you a point of focus to which you can return.

Another obstacle is the tendency we all have to come to scripture from the context of our own needs, or, rather, our own *perceived* needs. We may come to the scripture very much focused on the text, we may come very open and receptive to God, but we come with a very particular need. There is some crucial, burning issue in our hearts or a real burden weighing heavily upon our souls, and we bring this to the scripture and seek God's Word to be spoken into that need. Now there is nothing wrong with this in and of itself. But often, with the need, we also bring our desired solution. What we must do in such a situation is realize that we have to trust God to address us in the way *God* thinks best.

One of the things I have discovered, and I suspect you may have discovered this too, is that most of what I think are my needs are in reality symptoms. My needs are symptoms of deeper dynamics in my life of which I have not yet become aware. I have often discovered that when I pray to God about a need, God is not concerned with my symptoms; God is concerned with the *cause*. I have frequently found God beginning to work in ways that, at least on the surface, seem to me to have nothing to do with what I perceive as being my need. Then I gradually begin to realize that something has happened to that need. I awaken to the realization that it has been met, but not in the way that I expected. I was praying, "Lord, I have this need. I want you to meet this need in this particular way. Here it is, Lord, I am laying it before you." And the Lord does "exceedingly abundantly above all I ask or think." He treats the real need, not the symptom.

Now I am not saying that we shouldn't bring our perceived needs to God or to the reading of scripture. However, we should be open to the possibility that the real need probably isn't what we think it is. Thus, when we come to the scripture with the tendency to reduce the scripture to our need and seek in it a specific answer to our specific need, we may be closing the channels of our receptivity to the Word God would speak to us at a much deeper level of our being than the symptoms we bring. In bringing our needs to the scripture, we must be willing to receive the Word God speaks to us even if it doesn't seem to meet our perceived need.

Another obstacle to spiritual reading is lazy expectations or approaching our spiritual reading with the idea that God will use whatever we give, no matter how slipshod or lackadaisical it may be. This obstacle relates to an aspect of the spiritual discipline of scripture reading that we discussed in Wesley's guidelines: giving God the best time of our day. Whenever we begin to give God the "leftovers" for spiritual reading, our vital encounter with the living Word will become less and less frequent. We will also find that giving God the leftovers tends to generate most of the obstacles to spiritual reading we have been considering here.

Another obstacle, usually associated with giving God the leftovers, is inconsistency in the spiritual discipline of reading scripture. We may start off enthusiastically, giving God optimum time, being truly present to God in the scripture, and being open to the address of God's Word into our lives. Then something arises that causes us to postpone our time of spiritual reading until a more convenient point on a certain day. A day or so later we again postpone our time with the scripture. Then we may begin to miss a day now and then until, finally, our times of spiritual reading become the exceptions rather than the norm.

While we can never operate legalistically in the area of spiritual disciplines, we must resist with all our strength the temptation to make our spiritual reading a lesser priority in our daily routine. In the constant competition for our time and attention, nothing must be allowed to usurp the time we consecrate to God.

A final obstacle arises with our choice of location for our spiritual reading. If our physical location is one that is annoyingly uncomfortable, noisy, distracting, disturbing, or disrupting, our spiritual reading is going to be adversely affected. Different persons have different levels of tolerance in this area. Some persons can concentrate best, can be fully present and centered, in rather noisy and disordered surroundings. Most persons require an atmosphere of silence and order to be able to center down and be attentive to God in the scripture. Our particular personality type has something to do with this diversity. Here you must find for yourself that "space" in your life where you are best able to be present to God in centered, focused receptivity.

There may be many other personal obstacles that you will encounter in your spiritual reading. Those which have been given here are the most usual and general types of obstacles encountered. Usually personal obstacles will be related to these more usual and general types so that you may be able to work through your own personal obstacles to spiritual reading by seeing if they relate to one or more of the ones listed here.

One final word on obstacles. The emergence of any of these obstacles, or a combination of them, in your spiritual reading, may in itself be a crucial point of your spiritual formation. The obstacle itself may be a symptom of something in your life that is resisting encounter with God. The obstacle itself may reveal something reluctant to be addressed by that living, penetrating Word of God, something defending its own existence in your life by subverting the discipline of spiritual reading. If this should be the case, and often you may not know it is the case, then overcoming that obstacle by the exercise of a spiritual discipline of obedience at the point of the obstacle will open your life to God's work of transforming grace.

13.

The Practice of Spiritual Reading

*W*E come now to the practice of spiritual reading of scripture. We will consider some specific techniques of reading scripture that will enhance our spiritual formation. We will examine methods of coming to the scripture which enabel us to be addressed by the living Word of God. Before we begin our considerations, let us once again release ourselves to God for the work God purposes to do in us through this chapter.

Our heavenly Father, thank you for what you have been doing in our minds and hearts throughout this book. We thank you for the new understandings you have given, for the new perceptions you have brought to birth in us, for the new experiences of your grace and love, for the new possibilities of a richer and deeper life in Jesus Christ. Again we turn to you, our Father, seeking to be open and receptive to what you want to do in us through this chapter. Help us to be open to your leading into those techniques of spiritual reading that will best open us to your living Word. Amen.

There are three aspects of spiritual reading of scripture: approach, encounter, and response. In this chapter we will look at each aspect separately, but with the realization that in spiritual reading these form a trinitarian unity. The loss or weakening of any single aspect will have its corresponding effect on the other aspects.

APPROACH

All that we have been considering up to this point is associated with our approach to the scripture. This emphasis is as it should be; for our approach will determine the viability of our encounter and our response. There are two essential elements which we have considered in our approach to scripture: attitudes and structures. It might be good to pull them together here.

Attitudes

Attitudes relate to the posture of being we bring to the reading of scripture. This includes our views of self, the Bible, and Christian existence, as well as the formational and relational dynamics we employ in our reading.

View of Self. Spiritual reading of scripture entails an awareness that in some profoundly relevant way we are deeply and intimately related to the God who is proclaimed and portrayed in scripture. God who breaks into human history in the Bible is also radically involved in our own personal history and the history of our own time. We have described this as being a word spoken forth by God into the world, a word which, though garbled, distorted, and debased by the dehumanizing and destructive dynamics of the world, is, nevertheless, a word that God is seeking to conform to the image of Christ through the nurture of God's living Word. We must come to the scripture, therefore, as a word of God seeking to be addressed by the Word of God.

View of the Bible. Spiritual reading of scripture also entails an awareness that in the Bible we have something more than simply a human literary production. There is a dimension of the Bible which escapes purely human parameters. There is a dynamic present in the Bible which enlivens the human terms and phrases. There is a reality in

140

it that breaks through the human story. We have described this as the iconographic nature of scripture. Scripture presents windows into an alternate order of being, openings into a realm of existence that is radically "other" than the realm of existence that has garbled, distorted, and debased the word God has spoken us forth to be. The icons of scripture call us from our garbled value systems, from our distorted structures of being, from our debased dynamics of action and relationship into a value system, a structure of being, a dynamic of action and relationship wherein we can find healing, transformation, and wholeness. It is through the icons of scripture that we encounter the living Word of God. We must come to the scripture, therefore, as an icon in which we expect to encounter that living Word.

View of Existence. Spiritual reading of scripture further entails a comprehension that the value system, the structure of being, the dynamic of action and relationship revealed in the icons of scripture are something more than simply superficial variations of the values, structures, and dynamics of our garbled, distorted, and debased word. The realm of the Word is an order of being of such wholeness that it is totally destructive to anything that does not resonate with its wholeness. Yet it is an order of being of such life that it can breathe its life into the death of our old being and raise us up into its wholeness and life. We have spoken of this as kairotic existence. We must come to the scripture, therefore, with an awareness that our whole order of being will be brought into the presence of an order of Being that will ultimately challenge anything and everything in our being and doing which is not consistent with its wholeness and life.

Formational Dynamics. If we approach the spiritual reading of scripture as a word of God seeking to be addressed by the Word, if we come to the scripture as an icon that opens to us the realm of the Word, if we come to the text as an intrusion of the wholeness and life of kairotic existence into our brokenness and death, then we will be well on the way to approaching the text formationally. To bring our word to the icons of kairotic existence requires that we come not seeking to master the text from the parameters of our own order of being; not seeking to control the text for the support, defense, and advancement of our own purposes; not seeking to manipulate the text for the fulfillment of our own agenda in our own lives and the lives of others. Formational dynamics require that we come to the text seeking to allow the wholeness and life of kairotic existence to master us, seeking to allow the purposes of the living Word to be fulfilled in us, seeking to allow God to speak us forth into the world according to God's agenda.

Relational Dynamics. If the first four attitudes of approach to the scripture are in place, we will also be positioned for a relational involvement with the Word of God. We will neither come to the scripture as a means of manipulating God to do what we want God to do for us, nor employ the scripture as a means for conforming ourselves to what we think God wants us to be and do. Our approach to scripture will be one of realizing the text as the matrix of our entrance into relationship with God, as the context of our opening of ourselves to God in loving, responsive yieldedness, and as the environment in which God meets us in vital, transforming relationship and begins the work of speaking us forth to be God's word in the world.

Structures

If attitudes relate to the posture of being we bring to the spiritual reading of scripture, structures relate to the general framework within which our spiritual reading takes place. There are two essential structures for spiritual reading of scripture: spiritual discipline and practical guidelines.

Spiritual Discipline. In a very real sense, spiritual discipline is the structure which frames the essential attitudes discussed in the previous section. Those attitudes are basic dynamics of genuine spiritual discipline, but there is one additional characteristic of genuine spiritual discipline—the unconditional release of the discipline to God. Our reading of scripture should become an encounter with the living Word, a means of God's shaping of our lives. If this is to take place, then our reading must be an activity that we offer up to God consistently as a loving discipline released to God for *God's* use, on *God's* terms, in *God's* time.

We cannot view our spiritual reading of scripture as a means to any goal of our own devising. It must be a steady, consistent discipline we offer to God with no strings attached, no demands made, no expectations fixed, no limits set. We simply offer it for God's use or non-use. Thus, all the attitudes of approach to scripture are fitted together into the frame of spiritual discipline. Unconditional dedication of the discipline brings to fruition the attitudes of approach. In our spiritual reading of scripture we become available to God, open to the penetration of God's living Word, and responsive to the shaping of God's will for our wholeness and life.

Practical Guidelines. Here we need only summarize the essential aspects of Wesley's guidelines for the reading of scripture.

1. There should be a daily time set apart for the disciplined reading of scripture. This time should be: (a) set apart at the optimum point of our day, when we are at our best; (b) set apart physically in surroundings that are conducive to the opening of our lives to God; and (c) set apart internally from the pressures and tensions of our lives.

2. There should be a disciplined and regular coverage of the entire Bible. While it may take years to cover the whole Bible, we should develop some system (lectionary) that will insure our involvement with the whole of scripture.

3. A crucial guideline is the instruction to come to our reading with the sole purpose of knowing the whole will of God and with the fixed intent to do it.

4. We should, in our reading of any portion of scripture, relate the dynamics of that particular icon to the larger scope of kairotic existence that is revealed through the whole of scripture. In other words, don't lose sight of the forest while you are encountering a single tree.

5. Perhaps the most crucial guideline is the exercise of prayer. Prayer should infuse the whole practice of our spiritual reading of scripture: prayer that enlivens the essential attitudes of approach, prayer that activates the spiritual discipline of reading, prayer that keeps us open and recep-

tive to encounter with the living Word, prayer that consecrates us to obedient response to God.

6. Wesley's final guideline, in two parts, moves us from Approach to the spiritual reading of scripture to Encounter and Response. There should be, in our reading of scripture, an examination of our being and doing, of our hearts and lives. There should be an encounter with the living, penetrating Word of God. We will suggest some techniques for this in the next section on Encounter. There should also be an application of God's address in our being and doing. We will suggest some techniques for this in the section on Response.

These attitudes of being and practical structures make up the dynamics of our Approach to the spiritual reading of scripture. This mode of approach prepares and brings us to the point of Encounter.

ENCOUNTER

There are many techniques for encountering God and being addressed by God's living Word in the reading of scripture. There is also a wealth of resources available for guidance in this area.[1] In this section, we will describe some of the standard techniques for opening ourselves to the address of the Word.

In each technique, there are two essential phases: reading and hearing (or listening/meditating). The techniques are designed to enhance one or both of these phases. While these techniques are functional in their dynamics, they operate within the framework of attitudes and structures described in the first section on Approach. You must be alert to the danger of the functional dynamics of the techniques taking over and becoming the means *you* use to get God to address you. This is why I have placed such stress upon the dynamics of Approach to the reading of scripture. In a sense, if your approach is sound, then any technique can become a means for the Word to penetrate your heart and life. But if your approach is not sound, then the technique will become a means for the brokenness of your approach to distort the text.

144

The Techniques

The Meditative Technique. The simplest, yet one of the most difficult of all the techniques for reading and hearing is the technique of meditation. For this technique it is best to work with a small portion of scripture. This can be done either by selecting a small portion to begin with (a verse, or a brief saying or account), or by reading a larger section (perhaps the three lectionary texts for the day) and then selecting one small portion for meditation. In this technique you read the text slowly, carefully, with full attention on each sentence, each phrase, each word. When you have completed the passage, perhaps reading it through several times, you then focus your attention on God and become still, listening for God to speak to you. You might pray, "Lord, what are you saying to me here?" Then seek to be still and listen. If you find your thoughts wandering, return to the text, read it again, and still yourself once more to listen. There will be times when you hear nothing, and there will be times when, as in my experience, you will hear God address you with something like, "You are Pharaoh!"

Sometimes the focus of your meditation will be a single word or a single facet of the account in the text. At times God's address may lead you to such a point of focus. Once you have come to "hear" the Word addressing you heart and life, you begin the process of wrestling with that Word; you begin the process of meditating on what that Word means for what you are and what you do.

Let me share another experience with you. A couple of months ago I read the account of the anointing of Jesus in Mark 14:3–9. As I stilled myself and asked what God was trying to say to me through that event, God asked, "Did you notice that she broke the bottle?" A rather simple and seemingly "safe" question. But as I began to meditate on this fact, the Lord reminded me of one of the predominant spiritual cycles in my life.

The cycle begins when I sense the Lord pointing out something in my life that is precious to me (like the woman's ointment was to her—worth a whole year's wages) but is inconsistent with God's will for my wholeness. It may be

145

something very innocent, very harmless; but it is something I hold as precious and is thwarting my growth into wholeness.

The second stage of the cycle is avoidance. I try to avoid the probing finger of God at that point. I question whether it is really God who is pointing this out or whether I am not simply being hyper-critical about it. But God lovingly, persistently continues to point out the unacceptable presence of that precious thing in my life.

The third stage comes when I finally acknowledge that it is God who is speaking to me at that point. The third stage is the stage of accommodation. I try to bargain with God. I try to rationalize and justify the presence of that precious thing in my life. I try to get God to agree to let me keep it if I will offer something else at some other point in my life. But God lovingly, persistently continues to demand that I pour out that precious ointment at the foot of the cross.

At the fourth stage, I come to the painful, sacrificial point of repenting of that precious ointment in my life and pouring it out at the foot of the cross. After a period of apparent release, rejoicing, and renewal, however, I find that either this very thing returns or something else becomes precious in its place. Why? Because, although I poured out the precious ointment at the foot of the cross, *I did not break the bottle of self* which held that ointment as precious! My grasping, indulgent, manipulative self was still in place, seeking another "ointment" to take the place of that which had been poured out. Then I began to see what lay behind God's question, "Did you notice that she broke the bottle?"

This, I hope, illustrates for you the kind of meditative dynamics that operate when we find ourselves addressed by the Word. God's address is rarely the revelation of some propositional truth, some prepackaged morsel of eternal verities. God's address is usually very pointed, very personal, very practical. It addresses the deep dynamics of our being and doing. The Word "penetrates to the division of soul and body, to the inner dynamics and focal essence of our being, discerning the thoughts and intentions of the heart" (Heb. 4:12).

146

The Harmony-Dissonance Technique This technique facilitates the focusing of our reading and provides us the material for meditation. It is also a technique suitable for use with larger portions of scripture. You can use this effectively with the lectionary. As you read a portion of scripture, you keep alert to those things in the text that strike either a note of harmony or a note of dissonance in your thoughts, attitudes, feelings, or perceptions. Why this is particularly well suited for use with the lectionary is that if one of the three portions of scripture assigned for that day (Old Testament, New Testament Epistle, Gospel) doesn't happen to strike any note of harmony or dissonance, then it is likely one of the other two will.

Once you have finished reading the portion of scripture, return to those places where you experienced harmony or dissonance. It might help if you developed a system of marks you could place beside the text as you find those points of harmony or dissonance. On occasion, you may find that you encounter both harmony and dissonance in a passage of scripture. Open yourself to God at the point of harmony/dissonance. Let the experience of harmony/dissonance be the penetration of the living Word, opening you to the deeper dynamics of your being and doing.

What is God saying to you in that experience of harmony? What does the experience of harmony reveal to you about your inner dynamics of being? What does the experience of harmony reveal to you about your outer dynamics of relationship, action, and response? Is the Word addressing you at some unrealized point of your life where you are hungering and thirsting for wholeness and life? Is the Word addressing some area of brokenness in your being or doing which is crying out for healing? Is the Word calling to some deep emptiness that longs to be filled?

What is God saying to you in that experience of dissonance? Does the dissonance reveal something in your being or doing which is in rebellion against God? Is the Word addressing some point of your word that is garbled, debased, or distorted, to which you are clinging? Is God addressing some habit, some attitude, some deeply ingrained perspective which is inconsistent with God's purposes for your wholeness? Is the Word probing some dynamic of relationship that is not healthy? Is the Word penetrating to the heart of some pattern of reaction or response that is destructive to you and others?

These questions are examples of the kind of meditation that can take place at the points of harmony/dissonance. Here, too, as in the meditative technique, you need to still yourself before God and listen for answers to your questions. Again, remember that those points of harmony/ dissonance will tend not to relate to superficial dynamics of your being or doing. They may appear to start at the more surface level of your life; but if offered to God in openness and receptivity, you will find that these are points where God is addressing you at the deep levels of your being.

The Imagination Technique. This ancient technique[2] has become quite popular in recent years.[3] While it is a technique in its own right, it can also be used to enhance the other methods. In this technique, as you read a portion of scripture, you imagine yourself to be a part of the scene, a participant in the story.

You imagine the things you would be seeing: what they would look like—their colors, their motion, their size; the appearance of the other people, the expressions on their faces, their clothing, their postures, their movements. You imagine the things you would be hearing: the sounds of nature—the wind, birds, animals, the water lapping on the shore, boats creaking at their moorings; the sounds of human activity—talking, children playing, infants crying, people yelling or groaning, the sounds of work. You imagine the things you would be smelling: the scents of the surroundings—flowers, the sea, the earth, fields, barnyards, a carpenter's shop, a fish market, a baker's shop; the human aromas—perfume, perspiration, freshly washed garments, dirty garments. You imagine the things you could feel: the wind blowing around you, the stillness of a room, the roughness of a path, the textures of clothing, the coolness of water or a marble pillar, the heat of the desert, the wetness of rain or sea spray. You use all your senses. You let your imagination loose to recreate the setting of the passage of scripture.

Once you have recreated the scene in your imagination and placed yourself in the scene, then begin to examine your thoughts and feelings about the situation. Here again you may experience harmony/dissonance. This can become a focus for your prayerful openness to God and your meditation on what the Word is saying to you in this experience. You may ask yourself what you identify with most comfortably in the scene and then prayerfully meditate on why you make this identification. Or you may ask yourself what you would avoid in the scene and meditate on what the Word is saying to you in that avoidance. What do your negative and/or positive feelings about the scene reveal to you about your inner dynamics of being and your outer dynamics of relationships and your patterns of reaction/response to life?

This kind of meditative exercise focused on a scene from scripture can be a very powerful way to open ourselves to the penetrating Word of God. This process moves us beyond our minds with their rational, logical, cognitive, analytical approach to data. The imaginative process opens us at the affective, feeling level of our being where we often need to hear the Word of God. This technique can also be very frightening and disturbing. It may open up areas of our lives that we have been diligently keeping closed, even to ourselves. It may stir up levels of emotional response that surprise us. Occasionally, you may find yourself absolutely ecstatic with joy, or you may find yourself weeping uncontrollably as deep dynamics of your being are released in this kind of exercise.

Whatever your experience in such an exercise, open yourself to God in that experience and meditate on what God is saying to you through it. The same kinds of questions suggested for the previous two techniques can be used at this point in the imaginative technique.

The "If-You-Were-There" Technique. At first glance this might appear to be the same as the imaginative technique, and it can be used in conjunction with the imaginative technique. You leave the spectator stance and become a participant. Whereas the imaginative technique powerfully involves you at deep levels of your being in the scripture account, the "if-you-were-there" technique is somewhat less threatening—at least in its initial stages. We must remember, however, that in all these techniques we are seeking to be addressed by the living Word of God. We are seeking to open ourselves at every level of our being to the presence and purpose of God. This will ultimately threaten everything in our lives that is inconsistent with God's purposes for our wholeness.

This technique asks the questions: If I had been there, what would I have done? What would I have said? How would I have reacted? On which side would I have been found? Would I have had the courage to stand up on the unpopular side? Would I have gone along with the crowd? Another aspect of this technique is to identify yourself with the main figure of the account, if there is one, and then to analyze how you would feel, what you would think, what you would do.

Once you have asked yourself a series of questions such as this, your answers become the points of meditation before God. What do your answers reveal about the deep dynamics of your being? Is God addressing you at the point of your answer to reveal to you something in your life calling for God's healing touch? Take your answers to God in prayerful openness, and listen to what God may be saying to you in them.

In all of these techniques, you may find yourself being addressed by the Word in a way that requires a period of ongoing wrestling in prayer, meditation, and response. Rarely will you find that your encounter with the living Word of God is a simple, neat, clean, finalized solution to some area of need in your life. Almost always the Word addresses us at points where we need to begin to make a response. Over a period of time, this reaction can be used of God to make us the word God speaks us forth to be. The Word addresses us at very specific points of our being and doing, at the points where our word is garbled, distorted, or debased. God encounters us in the inner dynamics of our attitudes, perceptions, indulgences, manipulations, and values. God probes the outer dynamics of our habits, our relationships, our patterns of reaction and response to life. These areas are not susceptible to quick, easy solutions. When your spiritual reading of scripture opens you to some such probing point of encounter with God, you will find that that portion of scripture then becomes an on-going focus of prayer, meditation, and discipline until God's purposes for you at that point have been fulfilled.

These techniques are capable of being very highly personalized, as you probably realize. This is the value of such techniques. God's address is very individual, encountering you as you are, speaking to your condition. Any technique of spiritual reading that does not open your unique being to God is of little value in your spiritual formation. Techniques that enable you to hide from God behind a facade of religiosity will only increase the garbled, distorted, and debased nature of your word. I pray that you will use one or more of these techniques (or others like them) to open yourself to encounter with the living Word of God. But encounter then calls for Response.

RESPONSE

When our Approach to scripture opens us to Encounter with God, we have come to the point of Response. An encounter with the living Word of God calls for our response. This response should not take place simply at the rational, cognitive, intellectual level. The address by God calls for a response in the daily dynamics of our being and doing. This means that our encounter with the Word, our address by God, must be carried into the details of our daily lives. There are many ways in which the Word can be carried into your life. We will look at three of the basic patterns: Reminders, Disciplines, Journaling.

Reminders

Once you have been addressed by the living Word of God in a passage of scripture, it is of great value if you can keep that portion of scripture or the message of the Word before you throughout that day or the following days, or even the subsequent weeks. You will be consistently opening yourself to the shaping power of the Word if you are able to keep the passage or a reminder of the Word before you until it has become an integral part of your being and doing. Here are several ways in which this can be done.

Written Reminders. One very effective means for keeping the Word before you is to write out the passage of scripture or a brief phrase from it that recalls to your mind and heart that special Word. This can be done on a number of small cards, strategically placed throughout your "living space." If you place these cards at points in your living space where you are active several times every day, there will be almost constant encounters with the Word. One could be placed where you eat your meals, one on the bathroom mirror, one at your bedside where you will see it last thing before you go to sleep and first thing upon awakening, one on your desk if you work in an office, one over the kitchen sink or one on the door of the refrigerator, one on the dashboard of your car. Perhaps a large version should be placed on top of the television set! You could place one on the door you habitually use to come and go so that as you go out into the world and as you return from the world you will encounter the living Word. You know best the dynamics of your living space. Find those places which will be the most effective reminders of the Word for you.

What you place on the cards need not be an extensive quotation of scripture. Sometimes only a part of a verse will be all that is necessary to draw you into the depths of the passage that calls to the deeps of your being. On other occasions, rather than reproducing the text of scripture, you may want to use the focal message God is speaking to you out of that text. For instance, in my encounter with the Word in the Exodus passage, "You are Pharaoh," would have been all that was necessary to bring me back into the presence of that penetrating Word. In my encounter with the Word in the anointing passage, "Break the bottle," serves the purpose. Since the encounter with the living Word is a very personal experience, you will need to develop the reminder that will best return you to that encounter in the midst of your life. If the Word speaks to a particular activity, then the place of that activity is where you need to locate your reminders.

Memorization. This method can be used alone or in conjuction with the others mentioned here. The Psalmist repeatedly enjoins us to write the Word on our hearts or to hide it in our hearts, and then to meditate upon it there constantly.[4] Although written reminders in our living space can periodically recall the Word to our minds and hearts, memorization is even better. When we have committed the text to memory, it is there for the Holy Spirit to recall to our attention at all points throughout our day.

One of the ways we can facilitate this recall is to develop the discipline of remembering the passage when certain regular events take place. Perhaps you are in a setting where there are periodic sounds such as bells, buzzers, horns, chimes, etc. Develop the habit of recalling to your focused attention the text in which the Word is addressing you. Whenever the telephone rings, you can let it ring one or two extra times while you bring yourself before the Word. If you have a watch with an alarm or a timer, you can set it to go off periodically as a reminder to bring yourself before the Word. You can use the unexpected interruptions of the day as keys to bring you before the Word.

Again, you know best the dynamics of your life and your own characteristics. Develop your own reminders that will bring the memorized Word back into your consciousness. Here, too, if the Word is addressing some specific dynamic of your being or doing, you need to be sure that you develop methods of recall precisely at the points where those dynamics are operative.

Praying the Word. In a sense this is a variation of the first two methods or a method that can be used in conjunction with the first two methods. (The method itself is similar to the "Jesus Prayer.")[5] You develop a phrasing of the text of scripture or the message of the Word, expressed in a very brief prayer. For instance, in the Word addressed to me about the breaking of the bottle, the prayer, "Help me to break the bottle, Lord," would be suitable. Then, throughout the day, I would breathe this prayer to God as a constant offering of myself for the breaking of those grasping, indulgent, manipulative dynamics of my being and doing. I would especially offer up this prayer at those points where I found those dynamics operative.

Here, too, it is helpful to develop reminders to offer the prayer to God. Both the written reminders of the first method and the built-in reminders of your living space (bells, buzzers, horns) can be used to trigger your prayer. What you should seek in this method is a constant breathing of the prayer to God throughout the day, a constant opening of your heart and life to the living Word through which God can work in the dynamics of your living to make you the word God is speaking you forth to be.

Singing the Word. If you are even slightly musically inclined, you may use this variation of the previous method. We all have had the experience of having some melody or silly ditty get into our minds and then find ourselves humming it all day long. Why not use this dynamic for God's work in our lives? If you want, you can even use some tune that may be going around in your head. Simply put the words of the text, or the message of the Word, or the phrasing of the prayer Word to the music of the tune. If there is already a hymn or Christian song that effectively states the insight, you can use it as a steady reminder of the Word. If you use the melody of a popular tune or advertisement, then you will also have reminders through the day that will recall you into the presence of the Word.

In all of these methods of reminder, you are seeking to carry the living Word which is addressing you out into your daily life and activities. As you accomplish this, you will probably discover your need for the second pattern of response—Discipline.

Spiritual Disciplines

Wesley reminds us that when we come to the scripture, we should seek the whole will of God *with a fixed intent to do it*. The encounter with the Word of God is rarely a point of information. God's address to us seldom has as its sole purpose the enlightenment of our intellect. God probes and penetrates into those deep dynamics of our being and doing that are destructive to God's will for our wholeness and life. God addresses those things in us that are inconsistent with our being the word God is speaking us forth to be in the world and in the lives of others. The purpose of this encounter, the object of God's address is that we might be transformed from what we are to what God purposes for us to be. Our response takes the form of obedience—the obedience of spiritual disciplines.

We have already discussed the nature of genuine spiritual disciplines. The deepest disciplines of our lives are those that arise from our encounter with the living Word of God. These are disciplines that emerge from God's address to very specific dynamics of our own unique individuality. The spiritual discipline of reading scripture is a very general discipline and should be common to all Christians. But the general discipline has its very personal and individual counterpart in our own being and doing. As we experience the Word of God speaking to some aspect of our lives, we also experience some awareness of what God is calling us to do in our lives at that point. This is where our "fixed intent" to do God's will is actualized.

Perhaps the Word of God addresses some destructive habit in our life. Perhaps the Word probes some damaging attitude or limiting perspective. Perhaps the Word penetrates some manipulative dynamic of our relationships. Perhaps the Word lays bare some perverted pattern of reaction or response to the world. At whatever point we find ourselves addressed by God in the scripture, it is at that very specific point of our being and doing that we must begin to offer to God the appropriate spiritual discipline of obedience. The various techniques for carrying the Word into our daily lives can also assist us here, reminding us of the point of encounter with the Word, reminding us to offer the discipline to God.

As we noted, however, the discipline of obedience is offered with no strings attached. We make no demands on God, level no expectations on the discipline, place no conditions around the discipline. We simply offer the discipline up to God, day after day, week after week, month after month, year after year, for God to use or even for

God's non-use. We are not, by the discipline, transforming our being or doing in our own power. We are offering ourselves to God in the discipline to be transformed by God's power.

As we enter into spiritual disciplines, we will also experience the need for a support community to uphold us in the disciplines. Very few of us are capable of engaging in consistent spiritual discipline at this deep level of encounter with the Word. We will evade the discipline, rationalize a limitation of the discipline, water it down to a comfortable level. We need some structure of accountability both to hold us to the discipline and encourage and support us in the discipline. This was the genius of Wesley's Classes and Bands in the early Methodist movement. They were regular fellowships of mutual accountability, nurture, and support. If you have no way to participate in such a group, perhaps a spiritual director would be available.[6]

JOURNALING

The final pattern of response to encounter with the Word of God is journaling.[7] In the area of spiritual reading of scripture, journaling takes the form of our deep personal reflections on the scripture. It can be employed with all of the techniques described in the section on Encounter, and can also reflect on what has happened as you have sought to carry the Word into your daily life and to exercise the spiritual disciplines engendered by your encounter with God.

As you journal, take particular note of your feelings, attitudes, reactions, and responses to the Word. Analyze your attempts to carry it into your daily life, and the disciplines the Word has brought into being. Note your victories and failures, your elation and despair, your fulfillment and frustration. Be brutally open and honest with yourself regarding your encounter with and response to the Word of God. Keep it private. This approach will free you to write constructively. The only person who would ever see your journal would be one to whom you might choose to reveal its contents (perhaps your spiritual director).

Periodically, perhaps every two weeks or every month, review the entries in your journal. Look for patterns of response to the Word, patterns of feelings, sequences of victories or defeats, relationships between fulfillment and failure. Are these revealing something to you about your encounter with and response to the Word? Are there patterns of resistance to the Word? Are there certain situations in which your response to God is limited or nonexistent? Are there points where your disciplines are becoming an integral part of your being? Can you see evidences of the work God is doing in you to transform you into the word God is speaking you forth to be?

Reviewing the journal can provide insight into additional dynamics of your spirituality that emerge from your response to the Word. Reviewing may serve to reveal deeper levels of your being or doing which the Word of God is seeking to address. Often our initial response to the Word takes place at the more superficial levels of our being. We begin our response at the symptom level, not at the root of the problem. However, if our response is genuine, motivated by a deep desire to have God do his perfect work in us, God will use our response at the superficial or symptom level to open us to the deeper dynamics that need to be opened to the Word in responsive and disciplined obedience. Your regular review of the journal can illuminate those points where the Word is probing and moving us to a deeper level of response.

Approach, encounter, response—these are the three rhythms of the scripture in spiritual formation. The primary focus of this book has been in the area of approach, because this rhythm determines the quality and effectiveness of the rest. The rhythm of approach is the point at which we have been most garbled, distorted, and debased by our culture.

It is my prayer that God has used this book to lead you into:

1. A new perception of yourself as a word which God is speaking forth to be his in the life of the world.

2. A new perception of the formational mode of reading

157

scripture which opens your garbled, distorted, debased "word" to the shaping power of the living Word of God.

3. A new perception of the iconographic dimensions of the Bible through which the Word encounters you and probes and penetrates the deep inner dynamics of your being and doing.

4. A new perception of Christian life as kairotic existence, not simply a cosmetic rearrangement of the world's order of being, but a radically new order of being in Christ whose values, structures, and dynamics are "completely other" than those of the world. This is the realm of the Word which, in scripture, is spoken forth by God into your life to touch your garbled, debased, distorted word and begin to shape you into the word God speaks you forth to be.

5. An awareness of the relational mode of approach to scripture that allows it to become the agent of God's work in your life rather than your self-generated effort to work God's changes according to your own agenda.

6. An awareness of the being/doing dynamic in which your spiritual disciplines of reading scripture and obedience to the Word are not actions you "do" to bring about a change in your being, but acts of loving obedience you offer to God as a means for God to transform your being.

It is my prayer that these perceptual/experiential dynamics will enable you to enter more effectively into a regular and deep encounter with the living Word of God, using some of the techniques of encounter set forth here. I pray that some or all of these techniques, offered to God through your new approach to scripture, will open you consistently to the probing, penetrating, but gloriously transforming Word of wholeness and life.

Finally, it is my prayer that your new dynamic of approach to scripture, coupled with your developed techniques of encounter, will lead you into a response to the living Word that will enable God to transform you into the fully mature word God is speaking you forth to be in the world and in the lives of others. May God richly bless you in this great adventure.

Appendix A

Spiritual Formation and Psychology

A WEAKNESS in the popularizing of spiritual formation in recent years has been the proliferation of spiritual formation materials that seem to take the position that "one size fits all." Such materials present some program, technique, or method of spiritual formation. They imply that anyone who undertakes to fulfill the agenda will achieve mature spirituality. Formation, however, is a personal and individual journey. What works for one person will not necessarily work for another. This is not to detract from our earlier contention that spiritual formation is a corporate experience. We need the support and correction of others if we are to maintain consistent spiritual formation, but the specific nature of that formation is specifically adapted to our own uniqueness.

This raises one area which must be considered: the relationship between spiritual formation and psychology.

It should be made clear at the outset that spiritual formation is not a substitute for psychotherapy or counseling. Spiritual formation contributes to psychological wholeness and may contribute to a process of psychotherapy. Psychotherapy or counseling may also enhance the process of spiritual formation. Both are processes that seek growth into wholeness and, as such, can complement each other. In the process of spiritual formation, psychological problems sometimes emerge. If this should happen, sound psychological assistance should be sought.

Psychology does, however, have a significant role to play in enhancing our understanding of spiritual formation and particularly the development of our own individual program of spiritual formation. This benefit is seen primarily in the psychological understanding of personality types and the awareness of the psychological stages of life.

JUNG'S THEORY OF PSYCHOLOGICAL TYPES

One of the developments in psychology which has come to have rather widespread acceptance in recent years is Carl Jung's development of psychological types. Over the years of his research in psychology Jung noticed that people could be classified by the use of four pairs of personality characteristics. These characteristics relate to an individual's preference for a particular type of function in his or her interaction with the world. The four pairs are: Extrovert/Introvert (E/I); Sensation/Intuition (S/N); Thinking/Feeling (T/F); Perceiving/Judging (P/J).

In these four pairs, each person has a preference toward one side of the pair. We either prefer extroversion or introversion, sensing or intuition, thinking or feeling, perceiving or judging. This means that there are sixteen possible combinations of personality type. These are indicated by using the letters assigned to each function:

INFP	ISFP	INTP	ISTP
ENFP	ESFP	ENTP	ESTP
INFJ	ISFJ	INTJ	ISTJ
ENFJ	ESFJ	ENTJ	ESTJ

To indicate that a person is one of these types does not mean that the other side of the pairs is absent. An INFP, for example, is not lacking in the ESTJ functions but they are subordinate to the INFP functions in his or her interaction with the world. Nor does the designation of type indicate that all persons of one type will be exactly the same in their character or personality. Within each personality type there can be an infinite variety of emphases upon the relative strength or weakness of each element. For instance, one person may be an INFP in whom the I function is scarcely stronger than the E function, while another INFP may be extremely strong in the I function and correspondingly weak in the E function. Thus, in each type there is an infinite variety of possibilities.

Now, what do these pairs of functions indicate? Extroverts are essentially persons who find their source of energy in relationships with others; introverts are those who find their energy in solitude. Extroverts are stimulated by being with others; introverts find socializing a drain on their energies. Introverts find solitary activities such as working quietly alone, reading, meditating to be stimulating; extroverts find such activities a drain on their energies. Extroverts experience loneliness in the absence of others; introverts are likely to experience loneliness in a crowd.

Sensing persons are interested in facts and experiences, both their own and those of others. Their concern is with what actually happened or is happening in their lives and in the world around them. Intuitive persons, however, are interested in possibilities or probabilities. They are not as interested in what happened as in what might be or could have been. Intuitives are dreamers and visionaries for whom imagination plays an important role.

Thinking persons are those who make impersonal, objective judgment the basis of their choices; while feeling persons make their choices on a personal basis. Thinking persons tend not to consider their own or others' feelings when they make a choice but decide on the basis of objective, logical principles. Feeling persons, however, tend to make their own and others' feelings the basis of their choices. Thinking persons tend not to display their emotions openly; feeling persons are much more prone to public display of their emotions.

Judging persons are those who seek for closure in the activities of their lives. They like to "wrap things up." Judging persons tend to be highly schedule oriented and usually always meet their schedules. Perceiving persons are those who resist coming to closure. They prefer to keep things open-ended. Perceiving persons have difficulties working with schedules and deadlines.

All of this has profound implications for our spiritual formation. An extrovert will find corporate spirituality tremendously enriching. Worship (especially where inter-action with others is stressed), small group experiences, and sharing/caring types of spirituality will be very impor-tant to the extrovert. The introvert, however, will find soli-tary spirituality tremendously enriching. Solitude, meditation, monastic retreats, and reading will be very im-portant to the introvert. The same kinds of distinctions can be made for each of the other pairs of functions. In fact, the Center for Applications of Psychological Type, Inc. has de-veloped a broad range of materials relating psychological type to spirituality.[1]

The most significant implication of psychological type for our spiritual formation, however, is that if we are to move toward wholeness both the dominant and subordi-nate elements of our personality must be nurtured. Here is where much of our spiritual formation falls short. We tend to adopt those disciplines and practices of spiritual forma-tion which suit us. This means that we are, for the most part, adopting dynamics of spiritual formation that nur-ture our dominant characteristics, leaving the subordinate characteristics woefully undernourished. For instance, if we are an INTJ, we will tend to engage in forms of spiritual life and nurture that enrich and enhance those aspects of our personality, but the ESFP dynamics of our being will be largely untouched. This results in a serious and poten-tially destructive dichotomy in our spiritual life. The un-nurtured ESFP dynamics will seethe beneath the dominant INTJ and then "break out" in unexpected places and in un-foreseen ways, totally disrupting the spirituality of the INTJ dynamics. The personality type we have is part of what God has spoken us forth to be in the world. If we are to be the word God speaks us forth to be, if our word is to be shaped by the living Word, the *totality* of our being must be addressed. Our spiritual formation must open to God *all* the dynamics of our being.

If you are interested in pursuing this aspect of spiritual

formation, there are two possibilities you can pursue. The easiest is to purchase *Please Understand Me*, by David Keirsey and Marilyn Bates (Del Mar, CA: Prometheus Nemesis, 1978). This book contains a "Temperament Sorter" which will give you a fairly accurate reading of your psychological type. Although this book is not written from a spiritual point of reference, it does provide a sound understanding of basic human temperaments. It gives an excellent insight into the dynamics of each psychological type. The second option builds upon the first. In addition to reading *Please Understand Me*, you can take the Myers-Briggs Type Indicator analysis. The Myers-Briggs provides the most accurate reading of psychological type and is available through most educational institutions.

THE PSYCHOLOGICAL STAGES OF LIFE

Another psychological development, extremely helpful in spiritual formation, began with the work of Erik Erikson. He identified eight stages of human development and the critical conflicts native to each of these stages.[2] Gordon Allport continued this line of investigation in another direction, seeing human personality as a dynamic complex of characteristics in process of becoming.[3] Levinson's recent study in this area has focused on the midlife crisis.[4] Evelyn and James Whitehead have recently brought these studies of life stages together and related them to religious growth.[5]

The awareness of psychological stages of life and the formative dynamics of each stage is vital to holistic spiritual formation. Each of life's stages has its own agenda to be fulfilled. If we experience a "fixation" (an uncompleted task) at any stage, this will hinder our progress through subsequent stages and disrupt our spiritual growth and development as well. Also, certain stages of the spiritual life correspond to the psychological stages.

If you are interested in this aspect of spiritual formation, one of the best resources I have found is *Spiritual Passages: The Psychology of Spiritual Development*, by Benedict Groeschel. Groeschel describes the psychology of spirituality within the perspective of the stages of life and then provides an excellent analysis of the relationship between the psychological stages of life and the classical threefold path of Christian spirituality: purgation, illumination, union.

Another excellent resource, *From Image to Likeness: A Jungian Path in the Gospel Journey,* by Harold Grant, *et. al.* combines Christian spirituality, Jungian temperament dynamics, and developmental stages in an extremely helpful manner.

This appendix has not attempted to provide a detailed treatment of the relationship between psychology and spiritual formation. Such a treatment would require a book in itself and is also far beyond my capabilities. I have simply been trying to introduce you to a vitally important aspect of spiritual formation in hopes that you will pursue this area on your own, beginning with some of the resources noted. The main point is that your spiritual formation is a process of God's work in your life. Your formation is specifically related to the unique and individual dynamics of who you are and what stage in life you find yourself.

Appendix B

Excerpt from The Preface
to Wesley's Notes on the Old Testament

THIS is the way to understand the things of God: "Meditate thereon day and night;" so shall you attain the best knowledge, even to "know the only true God, and Jesus Christ whom he hath sent." And this knowledge will lead you "to love Him, because He hath first loved us;" yea, "to love the Lord your God with all your heart, and with all your soul, and with all your mind, and with all your strength." . . . And in consequence of this, while you joyfully experience all the holy tempers described in this book, you will likewise be outwardly "holy as He that hath called you is holy, in all manner of conversation." . . .

If you desire to read the Scriptures in such a manner as may most effectually answer this end, would it not be advisable, (1.) To set apart a little time, if you can, every morning and evening for that purpose? (2.) At each time, if you have leisure, to read a chapter out of the Old and one out of the New Testament; if you cannot do this, to take a single chapter, or a part of one? (3.) To read this with a single eye, to know the whole will of God, and a fixed resolution to do it? In order to know His will, you should, (4.) Have a constant eye to the analogy of faith, the connexion and harmony there is between those grand, fundamental doctrines, original sin, justification by faith, the new birth, inward and outward holiness: (5.) Serious and earnest prayer should be constantly used before we consult the oracles of God; seeing "Scripture can only be understood through the same Spirit whereby it was given." Our reading should likewise be closed with prayer, that what we read may be written on our hearts: (6.) It might also be of use, if, while we read, we were frequently to pause, and examine ourselves by what we read, both with regard to our hearts and lives. . . . And whatever light you then receive should be used to the uttermost, and that immediately. Let there be no delay. Whatever you resolve begin to execute the first moment you can. So shall you find this word to be indeed the power of God unto present and eternal salvation.

—John Wesley, *The Works of John Wesley,* 3rd ed. (Kansas City: Beacon Hill Press, 1979), XIV, 252f.

Notes

Chapter 1. Getting Oriented
  1. "Reprove and chasten" is what most translations read. But the Greek *paideuo*, while it contains the element of discipline (chasten), is a much broader concept of *nurture* into maturity or wholeness.

Chapter 2. How to "Read" without "Reading"
  1. Cf. chapter 5 for a fuller analysis of this mode of reading with respect to spiritual formation.
  2. Thomas a Kempis, *The Imitation of Christ*, paraphrased in *Deeper Furrows*, Errol G. Smith, ed. (The Washington Area United Methodist Church, 1976), 119.
  3. Matthew 11:15; 13:9 and 43, with the intervening statement of 13:14–16 which, citing Isaiah, indicates that the other hearers don't hear but the disciples do. Mark 4:9 and 23 (with the same statement as Matthew in 4:12), 7:16, and especially 8:18, where Jesus says, "Having ears do you not hear?" (Luke 8:8, 9:44, 14:35).

Chapter 4. Various Words of God
  1. Variously attributed to: Catherine of Sienna, Teresa of Avila.
  2. Thomas Merton, *Opening the Bible*, (Collegeville, MN: The Liturgical Press, 1970), 52.
  3. *The New Testament in Everyday English*, Don J. Klingensmith, (Fargo, ND: Kay's Inc. 1981), reads "All Godspirit scripture . . ."
  4. John Wesley, *The Works of John Wesley*, 3rd ed. (Kansas City: Beacon Hill Press, 1979), XIV, 253.
  5. Plural of "teaching" in the New Testament is used for the teach-

ings of human and demons: Matt. 15:9=Mark 7:7, Col. 2:22, 1 Tim. 4:1, Eph. 4:14 (has the singular but implies many varieties). The singular is used for the Gospel: 1 Tim. 1:10, 4:6, 13, 16; 5:17; 6:1, 3; 2 Tim. 3:10, 16; 4:3; Tit. 1:9, 2:1, 7, 10.

Chapter 5. Information Versus Formation
1. Aelred Squire, *Asking the Fathers*, (New York: Paulist Press and Morehouse-Barlow, 1976), 124f.
2. Merton, 6.
3. *Ibid.*, 24.
4. *Ibid.*, 25.
5. *Ibid.*, 33.
6. *Ibid.*, 58f.
7. *Ibid.*, 61.
8. *Ibid.*, 61f.
9. Cited in Susan A. Muto, *Renewed at Each Awakening*, (Denville, NJ: Dimension Books, 1979), 135.

Chapter 6. The Iconographic Nature of Scripture
1. Squire, 3.
2. Alan W. Jones, *Journey into Christ*, (New York: Seabury Press, 1977), 13.
3. Paul S. Minear, "Church, Idea of," *Interpreters' Dictionary of the Bible*, G. A. Buttrick, ed. (Nashville: Abingdon Press, 1962), I: 616a.
4. *Ibid.*, 616b.

Chapter 7. Kairotic Existence
1. Merton, 1, 7.
2. *Ibid.*, 27 (emphasis mine).
3. *Ibid.*, 44.
4. *Ibid.*, 46.
5. *Loc. cit.*
6. *Ibid.*, 47f.
7. Squire, 120 (emphasis mine).
8. Cf. Matt. 8:29; Mark 1:15; Luke 12:54–56; Rom. 5:6; Heb. 9:8–10; *et. al.*
9. Cf. Luke 21:7–8; Acts 3:19–21; 1 Cor. 4:5; Eph. 1:10; 1 Pet. 1:5–7; *et. al.*
10. Cf. Rom. 3:26, 8:18, 11:5, 13:11; 1 Cor. 7:29; 2 Cor. 6:1–2; Gal. 6:10 ("as we have *kairos*"); Rev. 1:3–22:10; *et. al.*
11. The Greek *asotia*—literally "unsalvation." Paul seems to be contrasting the dynamics of the two orders of being.

Chapter 8. Functional-Relational
1. Edward E. Thornton, "The First Lesson Is the Hardest," The Cessna Lectures, Asbury Theological Seminary, April 4, 1983. In his lecture, Dr. Thornton said:

As we look at developments in theological education and in pas-toral care, we see a steady move in this direction (prayer). The well-known Blizzard studies of the 1950's, broadly based re-search samples of ministers as to their view of what is most im-portant in ministry, focus, in a word, on the minister's *doing*. Thirty years later, now in the early 1980's, we have the even more immense and impressive piece of research that we speak of as the 'Readiness for Ministry' studies in which the high priorities for ministry, judged by ministers, seminarians, and laity alike, does not have to do at all with *doing*, but has to do with *being*; being genuinely obedient servants of Christ in our service of one an-other. In Clinical Pastoral education we have been moving in this direction as well. We've moved through the period of concentra-tion on what students must *do* when they go into hospital set-tings, then into a period of concentration on what they must *know*, . . . then we moved to concentration on what you *say*, . . . but in the more recent experience of all of us in the field today, we have been concentrating on *who one is:* on qualities of being.

2. Merton, 82f.
3. *Ibid.*, 83.

Chapter 9. Being and Doing
1. Merton, 64f.
2. *Ibid.*, 65.
3. *Ibid.*, 65f.
4. *Ibid.*, 67f.
5. *Ibid.*, 68.
6. *Ibid.*, 69.
7. *Ibid.*, 69f.
8. *Ibid.*, 70.
9. *Ibid.*, 72.
10. *Loc. cit.*, (emphasis mine)
11. *Ibid.*

Chapter 10. Breaking the Crust
1. George MacDonald, *Diary of an Old Soul*, (Minneapolis: Augs-burg Publishing House, 1975), 104.
2. Susan Annette Muto, *A Practical Guide to Spiritual Reading*, (Den-ville, NJ: Dimension Books, 1976), 26.
3. John Wesley, *Directions to Penitents and Believers for Renewing their Covenant with God*, 11th edition (London: The Conference Office, 1809), 11f.

Chapter 11. Wesley's Guidelines for Reading Scripture
1. Wesley, *Works*, XIV, 253. Cf. Appendix B for the full form of Wes-ley's guidelines, which are cited throughout this chapter.

2. A two-year lectionary is available in the *Spiritual Formation Resource Packet*, published by the Division of Ordained Ministry of the Board of Higher Education and Ministry of the United Methodist Church, Box 871, Nashville, TN, 37202.

Chapter 13. The Practice of Spiritual Reading
   1. The following are some resources for the techniques of spiritual reading: five books by Susan Annette Muto, *Renewed at Each Awakening: The Formative Power of Sacred Words*, (Denville, NJ: Dimension Books, 1979); *Steps Along the Way: The Path of Spiritual Reading*, (Dimension, 1975); *A Practical Guide to Spiritual Reading*, (Dimension, 1976); *The Journey Homeward: On the Road of Spiritual Reading*, (Dimension, 1977); *Approaching the Sacred: An Introduction to Spiritual Reading*, (Dimension, 1973); Morton Kelsey, *The Other Side of Silence: A Guide to Christian Meditation*, (New York; Paulist Press, 1976); Carolyn J. Stahl, *Opening to God: Guided Imagery Meditation on Scripture*, (Nashville: The Upper Room, 1977).
   2. Louis J. Puhl, *The Spiritual Exercises of St. Ignatius*, (Chicago: Loyola University Press, 1951). Cf. David M. Stanley, *A Modern Scriptural Approach to the Spiritual Exercises*, (St. Louis: The Institute of Jesuit Sources, 1971).
   3. Cf. Stahl and Kelsey on the use of imagination in reading scripture.
   4. Cf. Psalms 1:2, 40:8; 119:11, 15, 78; *et. al.*
   5. The "Jesus Prayer" has several forms: "Lord Jesus Christ, Son of the Living God, have mercy on me, a sinner;" "Lord Jesus, have mercy on me;" or, simply, "Jesus." The idea of the "Jesus Prayer" is to breathe this prayer throughout the day so that it becomes the basic rhythm of your life. For the classic account of the "Jesus Prayer," see *The Way of a Pilgrim*, trans. R. M. French, (New York: Seabury Press, 1970).
   6. For information on Spiritual Direction, cf. Adrian van Kaam, *Dynamics of Spiritual Self-Direction*, (Denville, NJ: Dimension Books, 1976); Francis W. Vanderwall, *Spiritual Direction: An Invitation to Abundant Life*, (New York: Paulist Press, 1981); Kenneth Leech, *Soul Friend*, (New York: Harper and Row, 1977); Tilden Edwards, *Spiritual Friend: Reclaiming the Gift of Spiritual Direction*, (New York: Paulist Press, 1980); Thomas Merton, *Spiritual Direction and Meditation*, (Collegeville, MN: The Liturgical Press, 1960).
   7. For information on Journaling, cf. Morton Kelsey, *Adventure Inward*, (Minneapolis: Augsburg Publishing House, 1980); Ira Progoff, *At a Journal Workshop*, (New York: Dialogue House Library, 1977); Robert Wood, *A Thirty-Day Experiment in Prayer*, (Nashville: The Upper Room, 1978); *Thirty Days Are Not Enough*, (Nashville: The Upper Room, 1983).

Appendix A—Spiritual Formation and Psychology
   1. The address is: Center for Application of Psychological Type, Inc., Box 13807, University Station, Gainesville, FL, 32604.

170

2. Erik Erikson, *Childhood and Society,* (New York: W. W. Norton Co., 1950).

3. Gordon W. Allport, *Becoming,* (New Haven: Yale University Press, 1955).

4. D. Levinson, *Seasons of a Man's Life,* (New York: Knopf, 1978).

5. E. Whitehead and J. Whitehead, *Christian Life Patterns,* (Garden City: Doubleday, 1979).

Robert Mulholland is Dean of the School of Theology and Associate Professor, New Testament Interpretation, Asbury Theological Seminary, Wilmore, Kentucky. He received his Th.D. degree from Harvard University in 1977. Prior to accepting his teaching post at Asbury, he was Assistant Professor at McMurry College in Abilene, Texas. He has also served several United Methodist churches in the Baltimore Conference.

Dr. Mulholland and his wife Lynn have two children, Jeremy and Tareena.